MW00445453

INDIE FILM *HUSTLE*

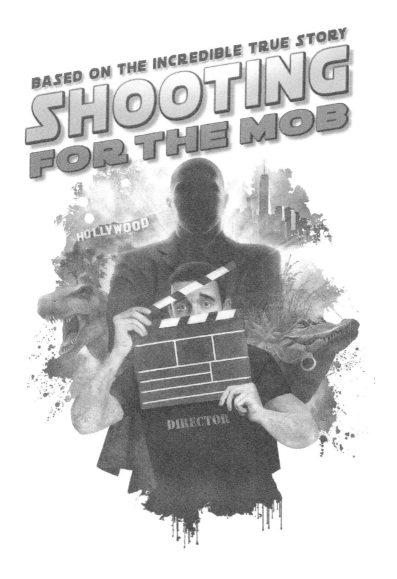

BASED ON THE INCREDIBLE TRUE STORY

SHOOTING FOR THE MOB

IFH BOOKS - A DIVISION OF IFH INDUSTRIES, INC.

Editor: Connie Deutsch
Cover Art: Dan Cregan

IFH Books - A Division of IFH Industries, Inc.

916-C W. Burbank Blvd. Suite #257
Burbank, CA 91506
www.ifhbooks.com

Ordering Information:
Quantity sales: Special discounts are available on quantity purchases by corporations, associations, and others. For details, contact the publisher at the address above.

Orders by US trade bookstores and wholesalers: Please contact the publisher at the address above.

Printed in the United States of America

Library of Congress Control Number: 2019930199

ISBN: Paperback: 978-0-578-72265-8
Ebook: 978-1-948080-71-2

Second Edition

For my girls —
May you always follow your dreams.

The book you are about to read is based on a true story. All the names of the people and places have been changed, except mine, to protect the innocent and especially the guilty. If you don't believe this is a true story, then I should get a fucking award for fiction.

— ALEX FERRARI

TABLE OF CONTENTS

FOREWORD

"This movie is not about me; it is about redemption."

— Jimmy

How far will somebody go to fulfill his dream of becoming a film director and making his first feature film?
Every person you ask will have a different answer, but I doubt that many could follow the path that Alex walked. He made a pact with a devil and sold his soul in order to fulfill his dream. What you are about to read follows the curious case of Alex Ferrari, a young aspiring director who undertakes an adventure in filmmaking like no other, and let me assure you, it is all true.

To many film professionals the moral dilemma of putting personal integrity at stake in order to get a movie made always happens at various stages in their careers. For Alex, it happened right at the very beginning. In a way, this experience that brought him to the highs and lows of his own personal and professional existence, was a trial by fire that either makes or breaks a human being.

Once he went through all of the turmoil and survived, nothing that came later in life matched the magnitude of sheer madness, and absurdity, associated with the experience of attempting to make the film *You Gotta Go for It.*

When you receive a call from a producer who is trying extremely hard to sound legitimate on the phone, but at the same time embodies all those gangster clichés from the small and big screens, you know this is *not* going to be a normal gig.

I was "fortunate" to receive that call at a point in my career and personal life when being adventurous was very acceptable and even desired. After my courteous and professional request to read the screenplay before committing to the project—and then getting hired on the spot, before I even had a chance to read it—I knew this project was going to be one hell of a ride.

The film business attracts the widest spectrum of characters like no other industry. That's what makes it so vibrant, unpredictable, crazy, exciting, and wild. The one thing everyone has in common is that they are all pursuing a dream.

Everyone on set may have different goals and dreams, but when the person at the helm of the film is following an ego-driven delusion, everyone's dreams can easily turn into a nightmare. Alex managed to navigate the stormy waters of *You Gotta Go for It*, even when it was clear to all that the film would never get off the ground.

Regardless of the insanity, the bond and friendship that came out of our adventure in movie making became something much more valuable that stayed with us for a long time.

This unique story is for anybody aspiring to break into, or already working in, the film business or anyone who is following a crazy dream. Even those who have no idea how Hollywood really works will enjoy this wild ride. It will energize some of you to dive in at full speed into the film industry, while others may run for their lives and stick with being lawyers, accountants, or doctors.

Regardless of what each of us takes away from this remarkable and unbelievable story, we should always remember that deep down this is a story of redemption, as Jimmy the gangster kept reminding us during this insane adventure.

— Boris, *the Cinematographer*

PREFACE

Truth is stranger than fiction. No other phrase better captures the story you're about to read, which, by the way, is based on true events. As unbelievable as it may sound, it has taken me over seventeen years to find the courage to go back to the darkest time in my life and write this book.

Many of us in the film industry chase our dreams relentlessly. We take chances that we shouldn't, get into situations that are sometimes reckless, and let ourselves be taken advantage of just for the chance at making our dreams come true. Whether that dream be writing, directing, or any art form, we all, at one point or another, allow our egos to lead our decision making.

You do need to have a dash of crazy in you to follow your dream, and that's what it takes: hustle, determination, and patience. All the greats who made it happen for themselves were crazy, but the one thing you can't do is abandon yourself, your morals, or your common sense in the pursuit of that dream. You cannot allow your ego to take control of the steering wheel.

For almost a year of my life I was trapped in a situation I couldn't escape. I feared for my life almost on a daily basis. I had no idea whether

Jimmy, the egomaniacal and bipolar gangster who hired me to direct his life story, would one day clock me over the head and throw me in a ditch somewhere. The amount of stress and pressure was incalculable, yet I didn't leave because, like any good con man, Jimmy was a master of dangling the golden carrot, and dangle that carrot he did.

I was flown to Hollywood many times to meet some of the biggest movie stars on the planet as well as billion-dollar producers and even the heads of Hollywood's biggest studios and talent agencies. I even got a chance to meet Batman. Yes, that Batman. You have to remember that I was a twenty-six-year-old kid, as green as they came. I had no idea how to handle anything that was happening to me.

Every time I would meet a movie star or a producer, I would say to myself, "Just hang in there a little bit longer. Just eat a little bit more shit and you'll get your dream; you'll get to your goal, Alex."

And by listening to that logic, I woke up one day and a year of my life was gone. I hope my story gives someone courage to leave a bad situation no matter how deep they might be in.

Now, this story is not all doom and gloom; it's hilarious, ridiculous, and truly unbelievable. Many of you will not believe parts of the story, but that's okay; it really happened. As Oscar Wilde said so beautifully, "When the gods want to punish us they answer our prayers."

Over the years, many people have asked me if I would change anything if I had the opportunity to go through this part of my life again. My answer always is no. This experience made me who I am today.

The main reason I decided to write this book was to create an account of one of the craziest Hollywood stories I've ever heard. I wanted to tell a story that would become an allegory of what *not* to do when chasing your dreams in Hollywood, or chasing your dreams, period. So, if this book helps just one person avoid pain, fear, and crushing disappointment in the pursuit of chasing his or her dreams, it will all be worth it, as cliché as that might sound.

When you chase any dream, whether that be in the film industry, writing songs, or opening up a business, you will be tested in ways you cannot comprehend now. That's the universe testing you to see if you really want it, if you're worthy of it. How you react to those challenges will determine if you achieve your dreams or not.

I made very poor decisions when that test came to me in the form of Jimmy the gangster. Those bad decisions are what make up most of this story. I hope my misadventures in Hollyweird not only entertain you but also help you along your path toward your dream.

We all have turning points in our lives. For some they happen early; for others they happen late. Some moments are painful, exciting, dramatic, fun, or life altering. But there are always life experiences that define who you are—and mine happened seventeen years ago, when I was a young and green filmmaker looking for my first big break.

This is what happened.

CHAPTER 1

Speak and the Devil Appears

You can almost smell the cancer oozing from the walls of this rundown racetrack that is decades past its prime. I walk down a long hallway, the floor industrial green linoleum. I come up to the service elevator, which looks like a death trap, and press five. The sounds of clanking and grinding as the doors close would make anyone nervous, but not me; I've been riding this elevator for seven months.

When the doors open, you can see the vast view of an aging racetrack from behind monstrous fifty-foot-high glass walls that protect the big rollers from the elements. Seats and VIP boxes stretch out as far as the eye can see. Beautiful race horses are training on the track outside with the Louisiana swamps as a backdrop. The carpets look and smell like something out of a fifties' Rat Pack casino. The furniture decorating my walk is frozen in time. I swear it feels like I just hopped out of a DeLorean with Michael J. Fox.

I'm walking to my production office, where I'll be having a major production meeting with the film crew for my first independent feature film. At the end of this long walk is an old closed-down cocktail bar. The walls are covered in blood-red flower-patterned wallpaper that would've been right at home in a scene from *Goodfellas*.

This is my asbestos-filled production office. Yes, I know, I didn't believe it at first either. Generally speaking, $20 million feature films with major movie stars attached don't have their production offices built out in a broken-down racetrack with alligators lurking on the outskirts of the fence, but it'll all make sense soon.

My crew are all sitting around old pushed-together cocktail tables. This is our version of a conference room. I say hello to my entire team: the director of photography, production designer, 1st assistant director, costumes, locations, PAs, and the entire gang from the second floor. This is a big day. We've been working toward the start of production on this film for over seven months.

I sit at one end of the tables, and on the other end sits the producer, Jimmy, a middle-aged, overweight man who looks like he came out of central casting for a Scorsese film. He's dressed in a red silk shirt and black dress pants. The thick gold chains around his neck shine in the lights. He is unshaven and smoking a cigar. Jimmy is not only the producer, but he's also the subject of our independent film. More on that later. As I sit down Jimmy says in his deep, cigar-smoking voice, "Our fearless leader has finally arrived."

"It's your world Jimmy; I'm just a squirrel looking for a nut," I reply.

The gang only gives a nervous giggle until Jimmy bursts out in hysterics; then the rest of the crew has the freedom to laugh.

I begin to run the production meeting. I speak with each department, answer questions, make decisions, and the meeting is going fantastic. My confidence is filling the room. I'm doing what I was meant to do—being a feature film director.

Jimmy is just sitting back and watching. He has been chasing his dream of making this film for over fifteen years, and this is his first real production meeting. I give all the department heads marching orders for the day, and I stand up and say, "Let's have a great first day of pre-production, everyone, and make a great film for Jimmy."

The crew claps before getting up and going on to their day. As I stand up Jimmy pulls me aside and whispers in my ear, "You did good today, kid. Really took control of the room."

Still flying high from the meeting, I say, "Thanks, Jimmy. It really felt good to finally get this film going."

He moves in a bit closer to my ear, and with a dangerous tone, he says, "Just remember who the real captain of this ship is."

He places his heavy meat-hook hands on the area between my shoulders and my neck, and he squeezes so tightly that I think my eyes are going to pop out of my head. He says, "I can always crack your skull with a shovel, throw you in a ditch somewhere, and straighten you out for good. I'm the captain of this ship. Don't forget that." He lets go and yells out to the entire crew, "Let's hear it for our fearless director."

The room starts to clap loudly, and Jimmy slaps me on my back as he walks out. I'm left there in pain, scared, and extremely confused.

Now, you must be asking yourself how a young filmmaker with no experience directing feature films got caught up with a bipolar, egomaniacal gangster trying to make a film about his life. I've been asking myself that same question every day for months now.

Before we get into this crazy story, I think it's important for you to know how I got here.

CHAPTER 2

The Film Nerd

Like many filmmakers of my generation, I was raised in the glorious eighties. My earliest thought of even thinking about being a filmmaker came to me on my birthday in 1982. We were standing in a long line that wrapped around the block in New York. My mother had taken me to see a film about an alien who comes to earth and befriends a young boy.

"What are we watching?" I asked my mother.

"It's called *E.T. The Extra-Terrestrial*," she told me.

I looked at the poster, which at that point was the only thing I knew about the movie, and I began to cry and act up in line. "I don't want to see that. That looks so boring."

My mom, in classic style, said, "Well, that's the only movie playing in this theater, so this is what we are watching."

I wasn't happy, but I went in. Walking out of that theater, my young life had been changed. Steven Spielberg changed it, as he did for so many filmmakers of my vintage. I ran home, busted open a notebook, and began to write my first screenplay, which went like this: *A boy is playing outside with his toys when he meets an alien. They become friends and play.*

That's pretty much it. I know, not the most original story ever, but give me a break; I was in second grade with no formal screenwriting education.

In 1982 there wasn't the same wealth of knowledge available now or even the awareness about filmmaking as a career, at least not in my corner of the world. From that day on, all I did was consume as many films and television shows as I could, watching on the small black-and-white television I had in my room.

VIDEO CITY

Filmmaking didn't really pop into my head again until I was in eighth grade. As a young and entrepreneurial man, I was looking for a job, but being fifteen was a major roadblock to actually getting employment.

I walked by the video store that we always rented our movies from and went in. I asked to speak to the owner and offered myself as a willing and hardworking employee. The owner took a liking to me and let me wash the windows and dust the shelves twice a week.

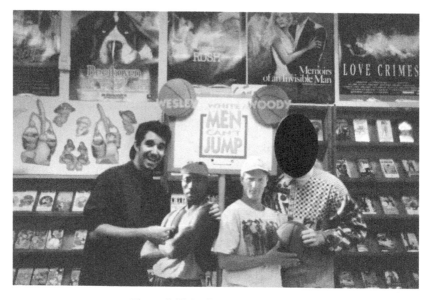

The good old days back in my video store

Within a year, I was the manager of the store. Trust me, telling twentysomethings what to do when you are fifteen is pretty cool.

At the video store I had access to film history. I would watch three to four movies a day. I always had a movie playing in the back of the store during working hours. Almost every night at home was a movie marathon.

You have to remember, this was the first time in history that filmmakers could actually study films again and again. Before VHS and video stores, filmmakers would have to wait for films to come back as re-releases in the movie theater, and even then you couldn't stop, rewind, and analyze a scene again and again as you could with the miraculous technology of the VHS.

During my high school years, I had a steady diet of Hollywood blockbusters, foreign films, and classic cinema. Then, one day, my grandfather gave me a Hi8 video camera as a birthday gift. I had no idea what to do with it, but I knew I loved it. I started playing around with it. I made short, funny films for friends in the neighborhood. After a few films, I had standing-room-only screenings at my house.

Editing was a challenge, so I taught myself the craft by using two VCRs. This was purely instinctual. I had yet to even read a book on filmmaking. I was teaching myself how to combine images to tell a story. This would be an omen on how I would work my way up in the film industry years later.

By the time my senior year was ending, people, including my parents, wanted to know what I wanted to do with the rest of my life. As I sat in my room, surrounded by hundreds, if not thousands, of VHS tapes and Criterion LaserDiscs—Criterion was the only way I could get those precious director commentaries I loved so much—I said to myself, *I seem to love movies, so I guess I'll be a film director.*

And just like that, I began my journey to become a filmmaker. Little did I know what a journey it would be.

FILM SCHOOL

So, now that I knew I wanted to be a filmmaker, I had to figure out what my next step would be. My mother said, "Well, let's look for a film school."

I was kind of blown away, as I really didn't think I could ever go to a school where they taught you how to become a director. We found a technical school in Orlando, Florida, called Full Sail. There I would learn many of the basics of filmmaking: how to wrap a cable properly and how to make a good cup of coffee during your first couple of jobs as a PA.[1] I kid. I did learn a ton from film school.

The one problem was that, when I went to school in the mid-nineties, the film industry was going through the beginning of a major technological shift from celluloid film to digital media. Much of what I learned in school was completely out of date by the time I got into the workforce, but I still knew how to wrap a cable and make a killer cup of coffee. Tuition well-spent, I say.

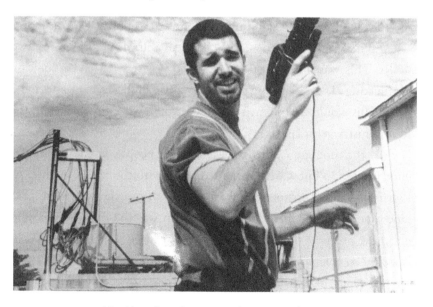

Me with my Super 8mm camera shooting some footage

---

[1] *Production assistant, the lowest position on a film set or production office*

While at school, I continued to watch films and expose myself to the new generation of filmmakers making some noise in the film business. I remember watching *Pulp Fiction* for the first time in the theater and having my mind blown!

It seemed that every day there was a new filmmaking success story you could dream about. There was Kevin Smith with *Clerks*, Quentin Tarantino with *Reservoir Dogs*, Steven Soderbergh with *Sex, Lies, and Videotape*, John Singleton with *Boyz n the Hood*, Richard Linklater with *Slacker*, and, of course, Robert Rodriguez with *El Mariachi*.

Robert's story was always special to me. A Latino filmmaker makes a kick-ass action film for seven thousand bucks in Mexico, then gets a huge Hollywood deal from Columbia Pictures at the age of twenty-three.

As a Latino filmmaker myself, who was only a few years younger than Robert, his path was the one I felt I could emulate to get me where I wanted to go. Trust me, I wasn't the only filmmaker who thought this way about Robert's filmmaking journey.

One day I found a rogue phone in the school that allowed you to call long distance—I abused that phone, but that's another story. I had the idea to call Robert up and see if I could get a job. I rang up Columbia Pictures and asked for the office of Robert Rodriguez. The operator connected me right away.

I couldn't believe it. Holy crap, she was actually connecting me. Moments later the line started ringing. I can't tell you how nervous I was. After a few rings, the voice message comes on and it's ROBERT! "You've reached the offices of Robert Rodriguez. Please leave a message, and I'll get back to you as soon as I can. Thanks." . . . *beep*.

I just started to ramble about how much I loved his work, that I had followed him and his story for years, and that I had read his amazing book *Rebel without a Crew* five times. I think somewhere in there I asked for an internship. I kept rambling for a while before I hung up.

Needless to say, I never heard back from Robert, and to be honest, I wouldn't have called that crazy kid back either.

For my generation, Robert Rodriguez's magical rise in the film business was mythological. It was the fuel that kept me going through the tough years that were ahead of me.

CHAPTER 3

I'm in Commercials Now

After college, I landed an internship at one of the largest commercial production companies in my area. My boss, Barry, was an alumnus of my school. Never underestimate the power of nepotism within film school alumni.

My only payment was gas money, which was nice since I had to drive one hour each way on a daily basis. Friends of mine didn't understand why I would show up five days a week and sometimes on weekends for no pay. I told them I was going to show up every day until someone gave me a job, no matter how long it took.

I was still living at home during this time, so I could afford to make this bold stance. Also, never underestimate the power of living at home after college. It really allows you the ability to do crazy stuff like this. Thanks, Mom.

After four months my shot at the "big time" finally came. Barry gave his two weeks, and the owner of the company, Stanley, literally said, "Who are we going to get to cover this job? Well, that kid has been here for months; let's give it to him."

So my persistence paid off, and boy, did it ever. I was offered a full-time position with a salary of $23,000 a year. I was so grateful for the job and the money.

My position was head of the tape vault, which meant I edited together custom demo reels for the commercial directors in the company. The time I spent at the production company wasn't all peaches and cream. Stanley turned out to have a mighty bad temper. I had never seen that side of him before.

He would yell and belittle employees, crew members on his sets, and anyone else who got in his way. It was my first introduction to an abusive boss. I swore to myself, when I was a director, I would never treat people like that.

When people act like that, it's generally out of insecurity and fear; an understanding that helped me moving forward on my filmmaking journey. I dealt with Stanley's abusive behavior, but mostly I just kept my head down and did my job.

During my tenure at the company, I watched hundreds, if not thousands, of commercials—studying techniques, styles, and executions. Any time a director would be in the office, I would pick his or her brain. It was an awesome time.

Then one day Stanley, who was apparently on his medication that day, came in and kindly asked me to check out the new room they had just built next door. I walked in and there she was—a brand-new AVID editing system. The system was running on a speedy Mac Quadra 950 33 MHz with twenty gigs of storage.[2] She was beautiful.

Then and there I decided I needed to learn this machine if I was going to be a director. For the next few months, with any free time I had, I would sit there and practice. I even paid to get certified by AVID as an editor.

After about a year, I decided to leave my comfy job and venture out into the world of freelance editing. Crazy, I know, but that's what you do when you are twenty-two. Luckily for me it worked out. I became one of the most well-known and popular freelance editors in my area. We were still in the mid-nineties, so money was still flowing.

---

[2] *Sorry, that was for all the editing and Mac geeks reading this book.*

My ego began to raise its ugly head, but more on that later. I was making mad money for a kid my age. I was still living at home, and life was amazing.

After a few years of editing, I decided it was time for me to make the jump to directing commercials. I was going to take the track that David Fincher, Michael Bay, and Spike Jonze took; I would become a killer commercial director, and then Hollywood would call.

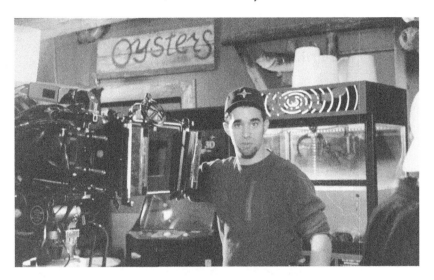

Standing next to the 35mm film beast while directing a scene from my commercial demo reel shoot

I had a good buddy who happened to work the tape vault at Propaganda Films, the worlds biggest commercial production company at the time; he would send me demo reels of all those guys. I would watch them again and again, studying every frame. This gave me the idea to put together my own commercial demo reel.

I charged up my credit cards with $30,000 to shoot five commercials on 35 mm film. Back then digital was still in its infancy, and film was still the industry standard. If I wanted to be taken seriously by the big boys, I had to have a big boy demo reel.

Since my ego was writing checks my knowledge and experience couldn't cash, the production was a bit of a shit show. I had a crew that had no business being on a professional set. My directors of photography—yes, there were two cinematographers—were corporate guys who had never really shot film. I hired them because they owned all the equipment and could get a film camera cheap—a mistake I would never make again. Never hire crew members just because they own equipment. Make sure they know how to use the gear first.

After that horrific shoot, I sent the film off to one of the best film labs in the country, who will remain nameless. I got a call at 6:00 a.m., which is never good, and was told that the processing machine had broken down and that I had lost a lot of my footage.

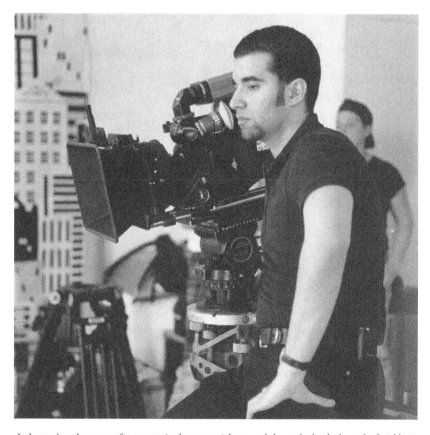

In heavy thought on set of my overpriced commercial spec reel shoot, don't ask about the facial hair

At the time I was devastated, but years later I realized it was a blessing. The footage was garbage. The combination of it being my first time directing a big job, and the inexperience of my cinematographers, was a toxic recipe.

So I called my grandfather and asked for a $20,000 loan to reshoot the lost commercials. My grandfather always supported me, and even though he had no idea what I was really doing with the money, he loaned it to me anyway.

I learned my lesson, hired a real cinematographer, a real production team, and we were off. The spots came out great. After I edited together the demo reel, I said to myself, *Wait 'til they get a load of me.*

Who did I think I was, Jack Nicholson from Batman? Seriously, my ego was growing out of control. I began sending out my demo reel to every major commercial production company in the continental United States and waited for the offers to come rolling in.

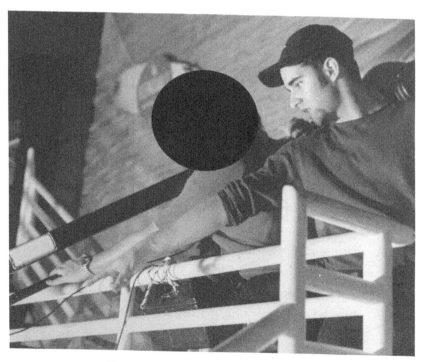

Directing a jib arm on the set of my spec commercial

Sending those reels out cost a ton of cash. The demo reels were recorded on industry-standard ¾-in. tape. Add in custom cases and overnight FedEx charges and the expense really added up. Of course, my ego told me, *I'll pay this credit card off with my first big commercial gig, no worries.*

Boy, was my ego wrong. I had no real bites on my demo reel. No one was willing to take a chance on an unknown director without a track record, especially one without representation who didn't even live in Los Angeles.

Considering that I refused to accept any editing work that was offered to me because I was a director now and needed to be available for potential gigs, the bills really started to pile up. Yes, I was an idiot. I swear that ego was killing me.

After almost a year of this, I was in major debt. I hadn't really worked a whole lot, and my dream of being a big-time commercial director was gone. I was in a bad place. The film business had given me my first big defeat in the battle to achieve my dream, and trust me, it wouldn't be my last.

ENTER THE CON MAN

When I said I sent my demo reel out everywhere, I meant it. There must've been five hundred copies of it floating in the ether. One of those reels fell into the hands of a local commercial producer, and I use the term "producer" extremely lightly. His name was Francisco. He rang me up and told me he had watched my demo reel and had a pro bono job for me to direct some charity commercials.

At that point, pay or no pay, I would have taken any chance to direct something. Surprisingly enough, the production went extremely well. There was a budget, a real crew, and we even shot on 35 mm film. I now had fresh commercials for my demo reel, and this gave a boost to my morale.

Francisco and I would shoot a few more projects together. I started getting calls to direct commercials, not big-time stuff, but it was work.

I even got a few jobs from the old production company where I started.

Things were looking up, and life seemed to be going well. I wasn't where I wanted to be yet, but I was on my way. Then, one day, I got a call from Francisco. "How would you like to direct a $20 million feature film about the mob?"

I was excited but extremely skeptical of the offer. Even with my ego a bit out of control, I knew the chances that I would get the opportunity to shoot a film with a budget of $20 million were slim, but that little voice in my head was saying, *This is it! This is your* El Mariachi. *This is what you've been waiting for.*

Francisco had a tendency to exaggerate, being an ex used-car salesman. Bad habits are hard to break, but I humored him. "There's this ex-mobster who is looking for a director to make a film about his life in the mob. He's a real dude, spent time in prison and everything. He wants to use a local director because he doesn't trust those 'Hollywood thieves,' as he puts it."

Francisco said he would set up a meeting at the post-production house where we were color grading our latest commercial. I agreed to meet him, but I really didn't think it would go anywhere. I had had so many meetings like this in the past. So much BS. So many "producers" who talked the talk but never walked the walk. Even in the few years I had been in the game I learned that much, or so I thought.

CHAPTER 4

Meeting the Devil

It was the next day and I was supervising a color-grading session in the big post house downtown. Francisco burst through the doors.

"He's here, he's here!"

"Who's here?" I asked.

"That producer I was telling you about," he said. "He's hanging out up front, by the client bar. I just showed him your demo reel in the screening room. He wants to talk."

I reluctantly got up and followed him out. There in the distance sat a middle-aged, overweight gangster who looked like he just walked out of a Las Vegas casino in the '60s. He was dressed in a gold silk shirt and black dress pants. The thick gold chains glimmered in the lights. He was unshaven and smoking a cigar. I said to myself, *This can't be real.* But, oh, it was.

Francisco almost skipped over to him, he was so excited. "Alex, may I introduce you to Jimmy. He's the producer I was telling you about."

Jimmy stood up and put out his hand. "Pleasure to meet you, Alex. I hear good things."

"Nice to meet you as well, Jimmy," I said, shaking his hand and thinking it was like grabbing a tree trunk. We sat down at the bar.

Francisco excused himself. "I'll leave you two movie moguls to it." And with that, he vanished into the color-grading suite, leaving the two of us alone.

"So I hear you are making a movie," I said, starting the conversation.

"Yes, I am," said Jimmy. "I want to make a movie about my life. There have been too many lies over the years about who I am and what I did. I want to make a film that sets the record straight. I did my time, and now I want to make something I can show my mother so she knows her little boy has done good. I left the life behind. It's really a story of redemption."

I sat and listened.

"I have a movie star attached already and have a few letters of intent from some others. The budget for my film is $20 million. The script is good but needs a little work. Could you help with that? Can you screen write?"

"Yes, I can definitely help with a rewrite," I said, thinking in my head how I could turn this into the next *Goodfellas*.

Jimmy continued, "I already had a Hollywood line producer breakdown the script and schedule it. I also saw your demo reel, and I have to say I'm impressed, and I don't impress easy, kid."

"Thank you, Jimmy," I replied. "Is the budget in place?"

"The money should be dropping any day," he answered.

Still not quite believing it, I asked, "Don't misunderstand: I'm not looking a gift horse in the mouth, but why are you looking for local directors to bring your film to life? Why not use someone from Los Angeles?"

Jimmy paused for a moment.

"Because I've been studying Hollywood for fifteen years. I've spent hundreds of thousands of my own dollars trying to get this movie off the ground. You have no idea how much I've suffered for this movie. I don't trust any of those fucking agents, managers, lawyers, studio assholes—none of them. I want a pure vision for my movie, not a vision that has been tainted by that fucking place."

You could tell he was getting heated when he started talking about Hollywood. "$20 million for a movie like mine is nothing. I can get that kind of money tomorrow if I wanted to, but Hollywood wants stars, A-list directors and writers. Fucking guys, they have no idea. Let me ask you something, kid: What kind of director are you?"

I paused for a moment to really absorb the question.

"I'm a storyteller, Jimmy. I tell stories. Story is the most important thing. Not the stars, not the camera, not the sets; it's all about story."

"Good answer," he said. "I'm meeting with some other directors later today. If you get the gig, I'll call you in the next few days."

I thanked him for his time and went back to my color-grading session. I didn't really think much of it. I'd had tons of meetings like that over the years, though never with someone as colorful as Jimmy. Those meetings never panned out. So I didn't think this one would be different, especially from a guy like Jimmy. Boy, was I wrong.

MEET ME AT MY OFFICE

I'm sitting in my apartment, editing some footage on my home editing system when my phone rings.

"Hey, kid, can you come meet me at my office?"

"Who's this?"

"It's Jimmy." He laughs. "Don't bust my balls kid, can you come?"

I was willing to see how this played out.

"Yeah, sure. Where is it?"

"Suzie's Diner on 5th and Castro. I'll be in the back booth. 12:00 p.m. See you soon."

He hangs up the phone. A diner? My curiosity got the best of me, so I headed over.

I walk into this diner, which was obviously built in the seventies. The smell of burnt oil with a dash of maple syrup filled the air. Jimmy was sitting in the back next to a gentleman I didn't know.

"Thanks for coming, kid. This is my office manager, Richard."

I shook his hand and had a seat in the sticky booth. There were papers all over the table. You could tell he'd been there for a while. Doris, the waitress, walked up.

"Does your friend want something, Jimmy?"

"Glass of water would be great."

Jimmy almost looked insulted.

"Order whatever you want, kid. Doris will take good care of you. You know what, bring him a BLT, and make it two. Richard, you want one?" Before Richard could answer, Jimmy said, "Just make it three BLTs, Doris. Thanks, sweetie."

"Glad you called, Jimmy."

"Sorry we had to meet here," he said. "I'm in between offices at the moment. So, look, I've decided to give you the gig. Do you want to direct my movie?"

I was a bit stunned. Could this really be happening?

"Yes, yes. I'd be honored to tell your story on film."

"That's why I picked you—because you told me you're a storyteller, and that's what this movie needs: a real storyteller. The name of my movie is *You Gotta Go for It*."

Jimmy pulled out a copy of the script and smacked it on the table.

"Here you go. This script has cost me hundreds of thousands of dollars. Read it. Let me know what you think and what you can do to make it better.

I picked it up and started flipping through the pages. Jimmy had mentioned that he had two major actors attached to the film—Oscar-nominated actor William Hurt and a young and sober Robert Downey Jr.

Jimmy loved the film *Heart and Soul*, which Downey starred in, and Jimmy said that he was the only one who could play him. Robert was coming up from the worst time in his career, and Jimmy said, "I wanted to give the kid a shot at redemption . . . like me. Once you read it, you'll understand where I've been, what I've done, and the price I paid. It's really a story of redemption. It has a *Count of Monte Cristo* feeling to it."

"That sounds amazing, Jimmy. I can't wait to read it," I said, putting the script aside to concentrate on what he was saying.

"Now, kid, I've already talked to the bonding company[3] about you, and in order for them to bond you as the director for this film they need to see how you direct a scene or two. I fought them on this. I told them I had all the confidence in the world that you could do the job, but what can you do? So we need to shoot a sizzle reel, kind of like a trailer with a few scenes from the script to show them you have the goods. I can offer $2,000 for the budget of the reel. Can you match that?"

I didn't hesitate. "Sure, I can do that," thinking that I had no savings and was barely getting myself out of debt, but I still had credit cards. This was my shot. I had to take it, right?

"Perfect! I knew I picked the right guy for the job. I have access to a great racetrack on the other side of the hill. It looks great. Perfect to shoot a few scenes. The owner owes me a favor, so we'll have the run of the place. Do you have a line producer that can help us put this thing together?"

"Sure, Francisco can help."

"Francisco? Do you think he's up to it?"

"Yeah, he's produced a bunch of commercials with me."

"If you vouch for him, I'm good with it."

For some reason when he said that I got a bit nervous.

Jimmy pulled out a box from under the counter. "I had these made up for you," he said, handing me a stack of business cards with my name and the name of the film printed on them.

You Gotta Go For It - Director Alex Ferrari.

"Now it's official: you are part of the family, kid. Go home, read the script, and let me know what you think."

"Thank you, Jimmy, for this opportunity. I won't let you down."

We stood up and Jimmy shook my hand. The grip was tighter than before. He looked me in the eye. "I know you won't, kid."

---

[3] *A company that guarantees the film will be finished no matter what, like an insurance policy on the film*

Doris came over with the BLTs. "Make one of those to go, Doris. My friend here has some work to do."

Just as I was getting up from the booth, another gentleman, looking like a poor man's Joe Pesci, walked into the diner and headed over to Jimmy's table. "I'll see you later, kid. My twelve thirty is here."

Dazed and confused, I walked out of the diner to my car. *Did I just get hired to direct a $20 million film about a mobster? Am I going to direct the next* Goodfellas? *Is this the moment I've been waiting for all my life?* All I knew was that I had a script to read and a shoot to prep for.

I ran home, sat down, and started to read the script. Jimmy's story was fascinating, but to be honest, the script needed a ton of work. I felt I could make something special out of it—at least, that's what I kept telling myself. Had I ever written a screenplay before? Not really, just some stuff in college, but my ego assured me I could handle a complete rewrite of this screenplay.

When you want to believe something so badly, it makes it easy for people to take advantage of you. I didn't know where this was heading, but the one thing I knew was that I had just strapped myself into a roller coaster and had no idea what was going to happen next. To be honest, that's what made it exciting and terrifying at the same time.

CHAPTER 5

Preparing for Battle

As I walked into the racetrack, all I could think about was Frank Sinatra and the Rat Pack. Jimmy was taking me on a tour of the racetrack. Along for the ride were Richard, the office manager without an office; Francisco; and Vinnie, the owner of the property.

We had already taken a look at the stables, racetrack, and boarding houses, but the magic was inside. There were five floors of production value just waiting to be shot. This was a virgin location that had never been shot for a film or television show.

While this was a down-and-out racetrack, you could tell that it had been magnificent in its heyday; however, business and attendance were down for the past two decades or so. While I was walking around, I thought this would make the perfect front for the mob.

The building was laid out like this:

First floor: parking, maintenance, and empty offices. Green linoleum *everywhere*.

Second floor: betting windows and the cheap seats for the horse races.

Third floor: more empty offices and a small restaurant that was still functioning.

Fourth floor: administrative offices, and you needed a special key for that floor.

Fifth floor: Here was the money. The entire floor was open to the indoor box seats for the high rollers. It was stunning. Daylight poured in from a three-story wall of windows. The mint-green carpet was something out of the '60s, I guess to subconsciously remind people of money.

Francisco told us that only a few floors were open to the public on weekdays, so we would have total control.

Francisco told me that the place he wanted to show me was at the end. As I walked down there, I couldn't help but look at the stunning view of the track and training area. You literally just had to aim a camera and hit record to get a cinematic view.

Francisco led me into an old-school smoking lounge. Everywhere I looked I saw red. Red floor pattern, red walls accented with mahogany wood trim, and even red metal ceiling tiles. It felt like I was going into Hell itself.

There were beautiful vintage wooden tables, antique-looking barstools, couches, and lounge chairs. In the front, there was a bar straight out of Scorsese's *Casino*. There were even small stained-glass windows on the wall. The production value was oozing off this place.

Vinnie told us that they never used this place anymore—we could have it all we wanted, and Jimmy boasted, "Do I deliver?"

I had to agree, and told him that it looked amazing and that it would take the trailer to another level, to which he smirked and said, "I told you so," and then he slapped me on the back and let out a huge laugh.

Francisco kept the tour going by taking us behind the bar to show us the kitchen and service area. This location was the gift that kept on giving. I was so excited. To recreate this kind of look on a set would cost thousands and thousands of dollars, and it was all here for us to use.

This project was getting off to a great start.

PUTTING TOGETHER THE CREW

Now that we had an insane location, we needed a few key people. First was finding an amazing director of photography. I reached out to Hugo, a Swedish commercial cinematographer whom I had always wanted to work with, and this was the perfect project to do so.

We met for coffee downtown and discussed the project. I showed him location photos from the track, and his eyes lit up. After a few sips of his espresso, he was in. We both decided to shoot on 35 mm film; again, there weren't many shooting format options back in the early 2000s.

Francisco volunteered to be the line producer of the shoot, so we had that covered. Once he was on, we started to crew-up quickly. We had sound, grip, camera departments, an art department, a thirty-foot crane for the exteriors, and we even had a Steadicam operator. This little shoot was coming along great, but I soon discovered that $4,000 was not going to cover it.

I called Jimmy and asked if we could go out to dinner to discuss the shoot and to update him on how things were going.

We met up later that night at a local seafood place that Jimmy recommended. I walked in and saw Jimmy sitting at a table, but he wasn't alone. When I walked over to him Jimmy looked up and said, "Kid, may I introduce my lovely wife, Carla."

We shook hands and she smiled and said, "I know who you are; you're the big-time director who's going to bring my baby's life to the big screen."

"I don't know about big time, but I'm going to do the best I can to do Jimmy's life justice."

Jimmy looked at me and said, "Justice. Funny word, *justice*. It means so many different things to so many different people."

I smiled and sat down. We ordered our food and a few drinks.

Carla was a well put-together woman. It seemed odd that she would be with a guy like Jimmy. I found out later that she came from old money, but still loved her job working in a hospital as a registered nurse.

After our waiter served our appetizers, Jimmy turned serious and asked me how the shoot was coming along.

I told him it was coming along amazingly, that we had a great crew, the location was awesome, but we had two small problems. "We still don't have a lead actor, and Francisco is having a hard time casting some of the other key actors as well."

He was getting angry. "Why didn't you come to me with this sooner? I'm the producer; let me produce. I'm here to help. I'll call my casting guy, Billy. He can get you everything you need. I'll reach out to him in the morning. He owes me a favor. I also know a few 'real' guys who can come by and act as extras."

I let out a sigh of relief. The term "real guys" had me concerned for a second, but I let it slide and instead said, "Seems you have a lot of guys who owe you favors."

His voice turned cold and he said, "That's how I get my business done, kid."

Silence. *Oh crap, did I offend him? Did I just screw this up?* Then Jimmy started cracking up. I started laughing as well.

Then came the tricky part. I took a deep breath and said, "The second thing we need to discuss is the budget, Jimmy."

Another silence. "What's wrong with the budget?" he asked.

My stomach clenched, but I went on. "In order to make the film look big budget, the cost is going up a bit."

Jimmy got serious. "Look, kid, I'm giving you a shot at the big time. I can't pay for everything and give you the shot. It isn't fair to me."

I could feel everything slipping away. "Of course, Jimmy," I said. "I completely understand, but I just don't have any more money."

The tension mounted, and he said, "Listen, when it comes to money for this shoot, think of yourself as an orange. Squeeze as much juice out as you can, and when you think you are done, keep applying pressure 'cause there's always a few more drops. I'll throw in another grand if that'll help, but this is your shot, kid, not mine. This movie will put you on the map. Opportunities like this don't come around often."

The vibe at the table was changing.

I tried to downplay it and said, "I completely understand, Jimmy. I'll figure out how to make it happen."

"That's what I like to hear," he said.

I changed the subject quickly. "So how did you two lovebirds meet?" I asked.

Jimmy turned to Carla and asked, "Can I tell it, babe?"

"Of course, baby. I love the way you tell it."

Jimmy picked up the story. "I had picked up Carla earlier and was driving along in my new Lincoln, doing the first-date chit-chat, when I looked over in a parking lot and saw a car. I knew whose car that belonged to, and it was parked out front of a massage parlor, and not a reputable one, if you know what I mean. I'd been looking for this scumbag for weeks. He owed me five large and told me he wasn't paying. I pulled in and told Carla I had some business to take care of and to wait in the car."

Jimmy was an amazing storyteller. He would have you on the edge of your seat with any story he told.

Jimmy winked at Carla and continued. "I walk in and told the receptionist that I was looking for my friend Tommy. He had forgotten his wallet, and I was bringing it to him. She told me the room number, and I thanked her. I swing open the door and see my good ol' pal Tommy finishing his happy ending. I grabbed him and dragged his deadbeat ass to the front, where I tell him to pay up or next time it won't be this pleasant. Then, I throw him out the front door window, naked and all."

My eyes were about to come out of my head.

Carla jumped in. "I was in the car right out front, and I see this naked guy being tossed out the window. Then Jimmy walks out behind him yelling something at him. Jimmy jumped back in the car. He still had pieces of glass stuck to his shirt."

Jimmy smiled. "Yeah, that was one hell of a first date."

They both laughed.

"I told Carla that night that I was married to the street, and she would always be second in my life. If she could handle that, then we could date."

"I told him that it didn't bother me. It's just boys playing with toys."

Don't ask me why I asked this, but the words just escaped out of my mouth. "So, Carla, at what point did you know you found the man of your dreams? Right before the guy got thrown out the window, or right after he told you you'd be second in his life to the streets?"

I really didn't realize what I had just said. I was caught up in the moment, in the story. Jimmy stared at me for a sec. The tension was thick in the air. I'm in the Joe Pesci "*How am I funny*" scene from *Goodfellas*. Then . . .

"You are fucking funny, kid," and both of them burst out laughing hysterically. Jimmy turned to Carla and said, "Love of my life, didn't I tell you this kid was great?"

Holy crap. I just dodged a bullet.

The food came, and we ate. Jimmy kept telling amazingly horrific stories like that the entire night. Was I scared? No, it didn't connect in my mind that Jimmy would ever do any of those things to me.

That was in his past. He was rehabilitated. I was still too ignorant of the situation I'd gotten myself into. As they say, "Ignorance is bliss," unless your bliss gets you thrown out a window.

Driving home that night, I was still so blissed-out that I almost forgot that I had committed to finding the extra money to produce the film. Keep in mind that I was twenty-six years old, wet behind the ears, and had never run across anyone like Jimmy before. I wanted to direct this film so badly that I could almost taste it. I didn't have the experience under my belt to tell Jimmy that my role in this project was as the director of the film and his role was as the producer, responsible for the financing of the film, which he just recently assured me he had covered.

THE BRITISH INVASION

We were still without a lead actor and had only two weeks left before we shot. Billy, the casting director, sent me a few headshots of some Los Angeles actors. Jimmy had already approved three actors for me to choose from.

One guy stood out, his name was Harry. He was an English actor who'd only been in the States for a few years, but he had already made a name for himself.

Harry had been a costar on a few medium-sized studio films, and the casting agent told me he was hot right then. I watched his demo reel and was blown away. The guy had chops.

Truth be told, at this point in my career I hadn't really worked with seasoned actors before. In the commercial world, the actors were mostly models turned actors. Working with real actors would be amazing.

I spoke to Harry on the phone, and we hit it off. We were both about the same age. He was excited to do the job and knew there wasn't much money, but we'd fly him in from L.A. and pay his expenses. Harry was in. We had our lead actor.

A few days later Richard, the office manager, dropped Harry off at my place. We decided he'd stay with me so we could rehearse and work out the scenes together.

Harry was a good-looking guy with a strong English accent. I'd never met anyone from the UK before—hell, I'd never met anyone from Europe before. I wasn't the worldliest person on the planet at twenty-six.

Harry loved to wear Hawaiian shirts. They were literally all he wore. We hit it off right away. This was going to be awesome.

THE TWIST

Everything was going great. We were moving along in pre-production. The crew was hired, and the deals had been made. Francisco told me he'd gotten everything under control. We were about three days out from day one of shooting.

I headed over to Jimmy's production office, which we had set up at the racetrack. I brought Harry along to meet him. Jimmy put on all the charms when he met Harry.

Jimmy said, "This guy looks nothing like me. I'm much better-looking."

The office laughed. Harry held his hand out, and with his full English accent said, "Pleasure to meet you, Jimmy."

Jimmy said, "I don't have an English accent. How's this thing going to work?"

Without missing a beat, Harry responded in a perfect Jimmy accent, "Hey, why don't you stop busting my balls, would you? I just flew across the fucking country to play you in this little film, so show some respect before I bust you in the head."

Silence. You could hear a fly fart in the room. Jimmy looked at Harry and burst out laughing.

"I fucking knew we picked the right guy. Holy shit, it was like I was talking to myself in the fucking mirror."

The room burst out laughing. I had given Harry some recordings I made of Jimmy when I interviewed him about his life. Harry had Jimmy down.

"You're good, Harry. Really good. Where are you staying?"

"I'm staying with Alex at his place. He has a lovely and very comfortable couch."

Jimmy looked at me.

"You're kidding me, right? How could you have our star sleeping on your couch?"

Jimmy loved to show off. This was how he operated. To outsiders he wanted to show he was the man. Rich. Connected. Powerful. Having the star of his film sleeping on the couch did not project that at all. He was a bit pissed off.

Harry jumped in. "It was my choice, Jimmy. I prefer to spend extra time with Alex so we can work out scenes, discuss the project, and make your film look amazing. I hope you don't mind."

"OK, if you're happy, then I'm happy. Richard, show Harry around and introduce him to everyone. I've gotta talk to the kid."

Jimmy pulled me aside and sat me down. "Look, kid, I hear things are going well."

"Yeah, Jimmy, we have a few loose ends, but we will be ready."

"Great. Listen, I spoke to the bonding company and they told me an eight-minute sizzle reel isn't enough. We need to add another scene to the shoot."

I felt like a bus had hit me.

"Jimmy, that's impossible. We are three days out from principal photography. It'll take a few weeks to set up a completely new scene, not to mention the cost."

"I know it'll cost more, so here's what I'll do," said Jimmy. "You handle all the production costs, and I'll handle all the post-production and editing costs. Deal?"

"Jimmy, this is going to be—"

"Kid, this is going to happen. The bonding company wants it, so I want it. This is your shot. Don't fuck it up."

Jimmy walked away. I was at a loss for words. How the hell was I going to make this happen? Setting up a shoot of this size is not something you do in three days. But this was my shot, right? I had to make this happen.

THE BREAKDOWN

The production team was in my apartment, which was home base for this production. Francisco was on the phone trying to lock down a few final things. We were able to scout and secure another location for Jimmy's requested scene thanks to our fearless location manager, Chip. More on Chip later.

I had never produced anything of this size and complexity before. Not only was I helping put this thing together, but I was responsible for the creative vision of the shoot. Thank God I had Francisco to take care of the major logistics. But I would soon find out that this project was too much for him to bite off as well.

Francisco came over to Harry and me as we were rehearsing and told me that he hadn't secured any of the vans or vehicles we needed for the shoot. I was stunned. It was noon the day before the shoot. What the hell?

He also hadn't been able to take care of booking a caterer or craft service,[4] among other crucial things needed for the production.

"What the hell, Francisco? It's noon. Why wasn't this done?"

"I'm sorry, man. I usually have my assistants handle all of that, and since we have no cash on this shoot, it fell through the cracks."

"Are you kidding me?"

I was livid. I looked at Francisco and could tell he was out of his league. Producing local commercials with a staff was one thing, but this was different. What pissed me off the most was that he kept lying to me about the progress of everything. He just kept assuring me with "All is good, brotha," or "I got this." But now, he just broke down. I'd ask him questions and he would be silent. The pressure was just too much for him. How the hell was I going to pay for this at the last minute?

All the stress I had been feeling over the last few weeks started to pile on all at once. I started to have trouble breathing. I could feel my heart pounding in my chest. I told everyone I would be in my bedroom for fifteen minutes and not to disturb me.

I went in, locked the door, and had a full-on panic attack. I'd never had anything like this happen to me before, so I assumed it was a panic attack, or I was dying.

This was my shot, and I felt it was all crashing down around me. Doubt started to creep in. *Are you ready for this, Alex? Can you handle shooting something like this?* That ugly voice in your head comes out at the worst times. I got in the shower with my clothes on and just let the water hit me. Over the course of the next forty-five minutes, I calmed down. I started to focus and think straight again.

I walked outside ready for battle. I got on the phone and started to pick up all the pieces. I just pulled out my trusty credit card and charged it all, adding more to the already-over-budget production.

I went and picked up the trucks and vans that night. As I was sitting there in the rental place's parking lot at ten o'clock the night

[4] *The person or company that provides the food all day for the crew on-set*

before a 6:00 a.m. call time for the shoot, I asked myself, *Can I really do this? Am I ready?*

CHAPTER 6

Let's Shoot a Trailer

It was the first day on set. We had set up our temporary production offices in a few empty rooms at the racetrack. I can still remember the smell of mildew in the air. God knows what we were breathing in.

My stomach was in knots. I was nervous but confident I could pull this off—I thought. As I walked on set, I saw Jimmy with a shit-eating grin on his face. He came over and gave me a huge hug.

"You up to the challenge, kid?"

"You know I am. Let's make this happen."

"Great, I have a surprise for you."

It was a bit early for a surprise, but at that point, I'd take it. Jimmy pulled out a huge box of t-shirts and hats. All of them said, "*You Gotta Go for It* Production Crew," on the front with a crew position on the back. The only problem was *all* of the shirts had "DIRECTOR" printed on the back. So you had production assistants wearing shirts that said "DIRECTOR." I can't make this shit up.

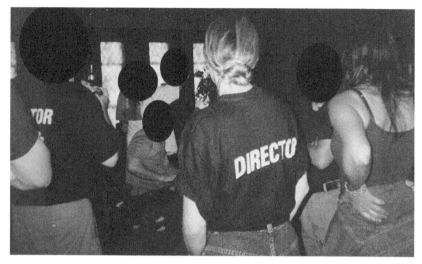

I told you, almost everyone had a DIRECTOR shirt.

What was I supposed to do, make everyone take off the shirts? So this is how we started the biggest shoot of my life.

Oddly enough, the actual production went extremely smoothly. Hugo and I were killing it. We worked well together. Shots were getting done. The crew was working as a cohesive unit.

We were out on the racetrack shooting some scenes with horses at the starting gate. We had an old-school forty-foot crane, where you have the cameraman and director sit on it. I'd never used one of those before. I have to say, it was very cool. I felt like Francis Ford Coppola sitting up there, getting my shots.

The images we were capturing were gorgeous from what I could see. Don't forget, this was 35 mm film circa 2001, so I didn't have the instant gratification we do today with digital. Harry was doing a great job, and the other actors were rocking it. We were on-time and budget.

All was good except for the script supervisor that Jimmy hired, Helen. She was seasoned but big-fish-in-a-small-pond seasoned. She was Jimmy's mole. He hired her to watch me and see if I could pull off directing the feature. Helen would question my shots, my coverage of the scene, and why I was moving the camera the way I was.

It was extremely irritating. At one point in the day, I'd had enough. I put her in her place and told her to please back off and let me do my job. It was all a test. Jimmy was testing me. By the end of the day, I had shot 112 setups—the average number of setups for a professional film crew is fifteen to twenty. After day one, I never had a problem with her again. She reported back to Jimmy that I had the goods and that she'd never seen a director move so fast in her career.

Strangely enough, Jimmy was not breathing down my throat on-set. He was in the background for the most part, or sometimes not even on set. He never said a word, just congratulated me on the first day of shooting.

DAY 2

On the second day, we had a fight sequence in the old casino. Jimmy told me he would find some good-looking extras and a few actors to play the wise guys in the background, but I didn't think he meant actual, *real*, wise guys.

When I showed up on set that morning, Jimmy introduced me to Vito, Carmine, Charlie, and dozens of other wise guys. Yes, I changed their names, but seriously, you can insert any name from *The Sopranos* for these guys and it'll work.

I said hello, and as I shook their hands, I looked down and saw that they were packing heat in their jackets. Not prop guns, real guns. I just smiled and kept going. What was I supposed to do? I felt like I was at an Italian wedding in the fifties, and I was the groom.

There must've been twenty wise-guys from different generations all over the scene. Some of these guys looked like they were straight out of *The Godfather*.

The gangsters were super excited to be there and hung on every word I said. They gave me all the respect in the world, even though the entire crew was wearing DIRECTOR t-shirts. If I told them to sit at a table and look busy, they would stay there all day and not make a peep. They just wanted to be part of the filmmaking process, which fascinated them. I imagined this was what Scorsese felt like during all of his mob films.

I swear, in so many ways, gangsters want to be movie stars and vice versa. For them, this was the coolest thing ever.

Vito was going to play the muscle in a scene with a couple of professional actors and Harry. As I directed the wise-guys, they fell into the scene as if they'd been acting all their lives. It wasn't that hard because they were playing themselves, which alone was kind of scary.

Later, I was sitting down at lunch and Jimmy came up and asked me, "How are my guys doing?"

"They are amazing, Jimmy. They really are bringing an authenticity to the scene, especially Vito."

"Vito is good people, but there's a few guys that were never seen again after they had a conversation with him years ago. He seems cool, but trust me, he's no-one to piss off."

I sat silently for a moment.

"Thanks for the update."

"I'm just kidding, kid. You watch too many movies."

He slapped me on the back and laughed. Jimmy loved to play up the gangster reputation. It really was a way to control people he wanted to control. I'd never been around people like this. It was crazy. I was living my dream, had every filmmaking toy I could think of, was telling a cool story, but the universe had thrown me a curveball with Jimmy. But I couldn't think too deeply on that. I had a shoot to finish.

The casino we shot in was old, rundown, and visually stunning. You just can't build stuff like this for a set. The production value was insane. We shot the fight scene, and it was coming along great. Everything was clicking. I was doing crazy shots from all angles and covered the scene in unique ways. I even jumped in a wheelchair with a handheld camera on my shoulder and shot a quick scene. I had to pay homage to director Robert Rodriguez and *El Mariachi*. All those

LaserDisc director commentaries were starting to pay off. I was in filmmaking heaven.

The next part of the sequence was shot on a Steadicam. It was the first time I'd ever used a Steadicam, and I loved it! You could float the camera around the scene, and it was smooth as silk. Cranes, Steadicams—what's next, helicopter shots?

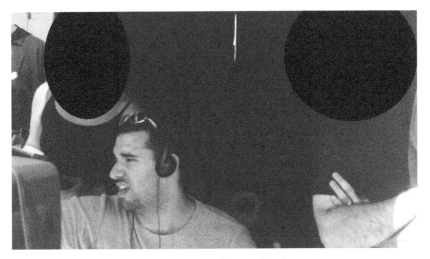

Me directing a scene for Jimmy's trailer.

Between takes Jimmy pulled me aside and told me that after fifteen years of trying to get his film made, he was finally seeing his story come to life on the screen. He started to tear up and then hugged me extremely tight. Then, he pushed me away and told me to get back to work.

Fourteen hours later we were done with the day's work. It was a long day, and the crew was amazing. I got most of the shots and coverage I wanted to get. We shot about 120 setups again—crazy, considering we were lugging an ARRI 35 mm film camera and dolly around.

At the end of the day, Harry came over to congratulate me on the day's work, and I did the same. He told me he'd worked with some big directors in Hollywood and that they had nothing on me. I don't know if he was being truthful or just blowing smoke up my ass, but either way it felt good to hear.

The next day was the last day of the shoot. This was the extra day and scene that Jimmy and the bonding company demanded. This had been so amazing I didn't want it to end.

DAY 3

We pulled up to this old, giant mansion that was just outside the French Quarter, where we'd be shooting multiple scenes. This was the day's carnival tent. Our remarkable location manager, Chip, pulled a rabbit out of his hat with this beautiful location. With only two days he had locked this place down. I swear he could talk the underwear off a nun.

The crew was all there, setting up for the first shot. Jimmy was in the breakfast tent with a handful of cast and crew.

"If it isn't our fearless leader. We going to make it happen today?"

"You know it, Jimmy."

"Good. It's just my life story, so no pressure, kid."

"I didn't know what pressure was until I met you, Jimmy."

Jimmy started to crack up.

The day's shooting went great. We had a few new crew members to fill up the last bonus shoot day, but all seemed good.

In the middle of a camera move,[5] I decided to have some fun with Jimmy. It was the least I could do after all the ball-busting he'd done to me.

I called Harry over, had him sit on the floor and start to meditate. I was going to tell Jimmy that production had stopped because of Harry, and I didn't know what to do. Considering he was an actor from Hollywood, Jimmy would buy that we had to stop production for thirty minutes for him to get his meditation in.

I ran downstairs to the production trailer.

"Hey, Jimmy, I have a problem. Harry has been meditating on the floor for thirty minutes and we can't shoot anything."

"What?"

---

[5] *This means that the camera and dolly are moving to another part of the location.*

"Yeah, Harry says he needs to meditate before each intense scene to get into character."

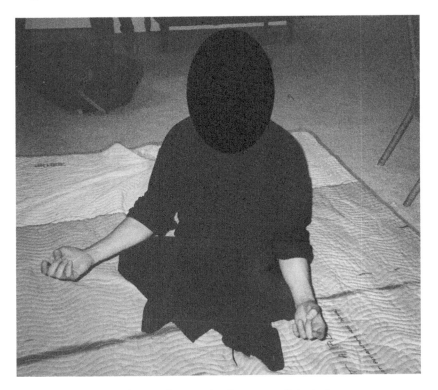

Harry mediating in-between takes about to get yelled at by Jimmy.

"Oh, I'll get him in character."

He got up and rushed upstairs, pissed off. When he got to the room, there was Harry, on the floor meditating with the rest of the crew sitting around watching him. Jimmy couldn't believe his eyes. He was pissed but had no idea what to do. He didn't want to blow up on the lead actor. It might get back to Hollywood that he was a crazy producer who yelled at his stars.

You could literally see the confusion on his face. Just as Jimmy was about to open his mouth, the entire crew, Harry, and I yelled out, "We got you!"

Jimmy let out a sigh of relief. "I was just about to crack some skulls up here. You're lucky, Harry. My next move was to get my baseball bat from my trunk."

We all laughed, but something told me he really had been going to get that baseball bat.

"Now get back to work, this is costing me a fortune." Jimmy groused.

What? This was costing *him* a fortune? I had charged up my credit cards to make this happen. I didn't have time to dwell on this; I had a shoot to finish.

We ended the day outside for one final scene at the other end of this insane property. I had the Steadicam guy start on a crane and then had him jump off, seamlessly continuing to follow Harry and some of his boys through the majestic trees.

"Beautiful," I yelled. "Cut, and that's a wrap!" Another fourteen-hour-day, but it was worth it.

From behind me I felt a cold rush as a cooler full of water was poured on my head. I looked around, and Jimmy was standing there with a few of his wise-guy buddies.

"Let's hear it for our director!"

The entire crew started to applaud and yell my name. I swear this was heaven. It was everything I had ever wanted. I got a taste of the dream, a small taste, but a taste nevertheless.

"Thank you all for such an amazing shoot. It was an adventure, to say the least. I'll see you all on the feature film. Thank you, Jimmy!"

"Thank you, kid! You made a dream of mine come true, all of you did. There's champagne and a bonus dinner waiting for all of you down in the meal tent. See you all at the premiere."

Jimmy came up to me and gave me a hug and a kiss on both cheeks.

"You knocked it out of the park, kid. I knew I picked the best director for the job. Now, enjoy tonight. We have a lot of work to do on Monday. I want this thing done as soon as we can."

And just like that, it was over. All those years of struggling while shooting and editing commercials and music videos had finally paid off.

***

The last day of any shoot is always the toughest for me. When you are on a film shoot as a director, you don't want it to end. Unlike writers, painters, musicians, or any other artists, directors don't get to practice their art often. It takes a crew, tons of money, and time for directors to actually direct. It's one of the most expensive art forms on the planet.

Not only do you want it to keep going, but you also start building a family atmosphere on set. The crew becomes your surrogate family, in a way. We are all carnies, and the film set is our carnival tent. We show up, set up shop for the day, do our show, and at the end of the day we pack up and move to another location the next day.

There's a bond you make during a film production that is hard to explain. When you see these people years later it's like no time has passed at all. It's the battle mentality; you all went through something intense together that you won't forget. The bigger and longer the shoot, the more intense the connection.

POST-PRODUCTION

Now the fun part starts: post-production. This is where I feel right at home. I get to see if what I shot is what I need to tell my story. I hope we got everything we need, but like any production there are always unpleasant surprises in post, and this production was no exception.

The raw film was sent to Los Angeles to be developed at a lab. Once we got the film back we went into a Telecine Room.[6] During this process, I sat in the suite and did a color pass with the color-grading artist. In those days, we color graded all of the footage, not just the good takes. It was faster and what I was used to doing for my commercials.

DI, or digital intermediate,[7] was still in its infancy, first being used the year before by legendary cinematographer Roger Deakins in the Coen Brothers' masterpiece *O, Brother, Where Art Thou?* Needless to say,

---

[6] *This is where film was transferred to a tape medium.*
[7] *The technology to color grade completely digitally.*

it wasn't in our budget, so we did it old school.

Then it happened. The first gremlin raised its ugly head. The footage we shot on the second day had streaks in the bright lights. This was a major problem and pretty much made the footage unusable. Since Jimmy was paying for all the post-production, I called him in to see the problem. He flipped out. He wanted to know how this could have happened.

We called Hugo and explained the situation. After further investigation, we discovered that the B camera, also known as the second camera, had a loose registration pin and the film was not exposed properly.

The post-production facility told Jimmy and me that they could try to fix it, but it would cost an extra $3,000 to do so. Jimmy couldn't believe it. He stormed out of the building. I could see him outside pacing left and right while he was on the phone. He came back in moments later and asked to talk to the manager alone. Five minutes later they came out and all was settled. The manager went down the hall a bit shaken.

The facility would finish up all the post, rent us an AVID editing system so I could cut the footage, do the final audio mix, and help us with the light flare issue in a visual effects suite.

"I took care of it, kid."

"What happened? How much will all this cost?"

"Don't worry, it's been handled. Now go and finish this so we can ship it out to the bonding company."

To this day, I have no idea what happened in that room, and honestly, I don't want to know. The next day, I locked myself in the editing suite and started cutting the footage together. I was so excited. It was working. Every scene clicked. We had more than enough coverage, and the performances were on-point. To be honest, it was the first time I really felt proud of my work as a director. I'd done tons of commercials, but this was different. This was filmmaking. This was storytelling.

As I sat there and watched the final cut I was elated. I couldn't believe I had done this. I had an amazing team of collaborators, and we all killed it. I sat there in the dark edit suite by myself and started to cry. This was happening. All the hard work, year in and year out, paid off. Now all I had to do was show this around Hollywood and the offers would come flying in—after I directed Jimmy's film, of course. That's the way it happens, right?

I'm being sarcastic, of course. Little did my ego and I know that the road ahead for me would be long and hard; this was just the beginning.

The next day, I brought Jimmy and his wife into the edit suite. I was a bit nervous. What if he didn't like it? What would happen? Well, we would soon find out.

They sat down on the couch and I pressed play. The only credits at the top said, "Produced by Jimmy and Alex Ferrari" and "Directed by Alex Ferrari."

The next eight minutes felt like an eternity. When it finished there was silence in the room. Holy crap, he didn't like it. Jimmy stood up looking serious.

"Well, kid, you gave it your best shot."

I felt like throwing up.

"And you killed it. Holy shit, that was amazing!"

Jimmy and his wife both came over and gave me a hug.

"You absolutely killed it. Scorsese would be proud. Actually, I'm going to have some of my pals reach out to Marty to make sure he sees this. You brought my life to the big screen."

Jimmy seemed happy with the cut, which was a huge relief. Now all we had to do was finish up the sound, music, and fix the light flare issue in visual effects. It was all coming together. Next stop was the big premiere for the cast and crew.

TRUE COLORS REVEALED

Harry flew back into town to see how the film came out, and he was crashing at my place. I purposely didn't let him see anything. I wanted him to be surprised with the rest of the gang.

Francisco gave me a call a few hours before the premiere and told me that Jimmy loved the film, but he wanted me to remove my name as a producer in the opening credits. He wanted the solo producing credit. What the hell?

After everything I went through to make this fucking project happen, he was going to take away my producer credit? I fucking produced this thing. I paid for the production. He "paid" for the post-production. We were both producers.

"I know, man," said Francisco. "But he said it would be fine for the screening tonight, but it would have to be changed before he sends it all over Hollywood. What are you going to do, fight with Jimmy?"

"That's exactly what I'm going to do," I replied.

I hung up the phone and started dialing Jimmy. Harry walked in and asked if everything was all right. I shook my head no and waited for Jimmy to pick up.

"Yeah, kid, you excited for tonight?"

"Hey, Jimmy, Francisco just called me and told me you want to take my producing credit off the film. Is that true?"

"Yes, I'm the only producer on this project, unless you want to pony up $20 million for the budget."

"Jimmy, I busted my ass on this project and I—"

Jimmy cut me off and started to yell at the top of his lungs.

"And what the fuck do you think I've been doing for the last fifteen fucking years, huh? You come in and spend a few days and dollars shooting some scenes and you think you caught up with me, kid? Let me tell you fucking something, as long as there is fucking breath in my lungs, I'll be the only fucking producer on this film. You hear me, mutha fucker? Don't you ever fuckin' cross me again. I've killed people for less than this. I run this mutha fucker. You are just an employee. I'm giving you your shot. Don't you fuckin' forget that. Do you understand?"

I was quiet.

"Do you understand, mother fucker? 'Cause if you don't, make sure to check your car for snakes under the driver seat, or that your brakes work for the rest of your mutha-fuckin' life. Don't cross me, kid. Don't fuckin' do it, or I'll crack you in the head with my Louisville Slugger and dump you in the bayou for the alligators. You get me? Do you fucking get me?"

I was in absolute shock.

"Yes, I get you, Jimmy."

"Good, I'll see you tonight, you ungrateful little shit."

No one had ever spoken to me like that. I had no idea what to do. Harry heard the entire thing. The man on the phone was not the fun, easygoing guy we all had worked with on set. Jimmy had finally shown his true colors.

"You OK, Alex? Was that Jimmy?"

"Yeah."

"What the fuck happened, mate?"

"I have no idea."

I called Francisco and explained what had happened. I told him I was not going to the screening and I was definitely not going to direct this guy's film. Fuck it. I'm not going to put up with this guy yelling empty threats at me.

Francisco, seeing that his meal ticket was about to walk, tried to convince me to go to the screening and stay on as the director. Francisco knew that if I left, Jimmy would have no more use for him and would kick him to the curb.

He told me that Jimmy's threats were not empty. Jimmy was the real deal and he was *not* rehabilitated. He was still running in deep circles.

"Just do what he says, man. I don't want to see you get hurt, or worse," said Francisco.

For the first time in this entire journey, I became scared, fucking scared. What was I supposed to do? Not show up tonight to the screening, leave the project and embarrass a gangster in front of all his gangster friends?

You have to understand, the only reference I had to mobsters and gangsters was the movies. I'd never been involved with a real wise guy, and that truth hit me like a bag of bricks. I was young, inexperienced about life, and not street smart at all. I had traveled to the deep end of the pool, and I was starting to have a rough time staying afloat.

TROUBLE IN LITTLE ITALY

Harry and I showed up at an Italian restaurant downtown. When I walked in, I felt like I was in a scene from *Donnie Brasco*. Wise guys everywhere. Red flower-patterned carpets, the smell of stale cigars in the air, and, of course, dark mahogany tables, seats, and blood-red booths.

I saw my cast and crew sitting in the back where there was a small screen set up for the viewing. I told Harry to join the rest of the gang. Francisco came running up.

"Thank God you came," said Francisco. "Jimmy has been asking about you."

"I'm here."

Jimmy walked over with a shit-eating grin on his face and waved Francisco away.

"Do we have an understanding, kid?"

"Yeah, Jimmy, we do."

"Good. I didn't want to get like that, but I can't have my star director not showing up to the premiere, can I?"

"Of course not."

"You know I love yah, kid. Stay in line, do your job, and all will be fine."

He pulled me to the corner of the bar. "Listen, I've watched this damn sizzle reel about a hundred times, and I have to say, you have the goods, kid."

"Thanks, Jimmy."

"No bullshit, you do. I want to be your agent."

I was still in a daze from what had happened and what was happening. *Did he just say that he wants to be my agent?*

"I was the agent for actors before, and I took good care of them. I know I can do wonders for your career too. Hell, I've already gotten you a huge directing gig." Jimmy laughed loudly with his Montecristo cigar hanging from his mouth. "So, are you in, kid?"

I had no defenses, no fight left. I was a broken soul.

"Sure, Jimmy, that would be great."

A wicked smile danced across his face. "Great. Now let's show everyone your masterpiece."

We walked over to the gang, who were all patiently waiting for the show to start. I felt like it was all happening in slow motion. Jimmy introduced the film, and I followed with a few words. I swear, I don't even remember what I said. It's all a blur.

Ten minutes later, the film was done. I got a standing ovation. Jimmy came back up to the front and said a few words about how amazing the experience was and thanked me for a job well done. He started showing me off and introducing me to all his wise-guy pals.

The cast and crew all came up to congratulate me. I was shaking hands and hugging the crew, but I wasn't really there. It was almost like I was having an out-of-body experience. One thing stood out: I remember Harry looking at me with a concerned look on his face. Francisco and he were the only others who knew the truth about Jimmy.

I'll never forget the look in Jimmy's eyes when he saw me walk in that night. "I got this mother fucker in the palm of my hands" flashed like a Las Vegas neon sign across his eyes. He broke me like a horse trainer does a young stallion. He had me. I knew it, and he knew it. I was in.

If there was a moment I could've left this nightmare, that night would have been it, but fear, manipulation, and inexperience got the best of me. Allowing my ego to lead the way had gotten me into one hell of a mess. That was my chance to get out, and I didn't take it. The world I lived in did not prepare me for a Jimmy—hell, most people aren't prepared for a Jimmy.

This was the beginning of the twelve-month odyssey with euphoric highs and devastating lows that would change my life forever. I was on this ride until the end, whether I liked it or not.

CHAPTER 7

Setting Up Shop

Since we had such a great experience at the racetrack shooting the sizzle reel, Jimmy was able to negotiate for office space there. Jimmy was happy as hell. He finally moved out of the diner's corner booth. We were given some empty rooms on the bottom floor. The rooms were very industrial-looking. Think David Fincher's *Zodiac* when they interrogated their lead suspect. The sounds of clacking and the grinding of old machines penetrated the wall. And what the hell was that smell?

Jimmy brought on Sid, an old accountant from New York. He had been a production accountant back in the day, but was well past his expiration date. Sid would work on the budget of the film for free. I guess being in the office gave him something to do in his retirement. Honestly, I think Jimmy brought him on to have someone to talk to all day. And of course, Richard, Jimmy's faithful office manager, was there. He finally had an office to actually manage.

In the early weeks of the office, Jimmy literally just sat around waiting for the phone to ring. I went to visit the offices once or twice but didn't move in. It was boring as hell. Nothing to do, so I stayed home. Every time I'd show up Jimmy would bust my balls. "Look, it's our fearless director who's never here."

I didn't care. I was busy at home working on rewriting the script. I sat Jimmy down and did a series of interviews to help me with the rewrites. As he told his stories about being in the mob, chills ran up my spine. Each story became more and more horrific. He would laugh out loud about beating up people, cracking kneecaps, and worse.

When giving me notes on the rewrite of the script Jimmy would always say, "This is a story of redemption."

I'm not sure what kind of redemption he was talking about, but I just nodded and kept writing. I rewrote that script for a month or so. I felt I nailed it. Jimmy read it and loved it. When I asked for a screenwriting credit, he shot me down. "I can't do that, kid. The original screenwriter is WGA, and I don't want any issues with them and my movie."

"But I literally rewrote 80 percent of the screenplay Jimmy."

"Doesn't matter. I can't do it."

And that was the end of the conversation. At this point, I would be happy just getting a credit for directing the film. I think this was Jimmy's plan all along. He would beat you down to control and use you as he saw fit. You could see that in Richard's eyes. He'd been with Jimmy for five years on this nutty, acid trip of a film project.

HOLLYWOOD

As promised, Jimmy started to build press kits for the film to ship out to anyone and everyone in Hollywood. This included a VHS copy of the sizzle reel. Day after day, Richard and Bert sent dozens of these packages out. Once I saw that there was some action happening at the offices, I finally moved in.

"Finally, our director has graced us with his presence. Since you are here, I have something for you." Jimmy reached under his desk and pulled out a director's bag/binder. It was beautiful. I'd always seen these on big movie sets, and now I had one of my own.

"Look at the front of it," Jimmy said, turning the bag/binder around so that I had a better view of it.

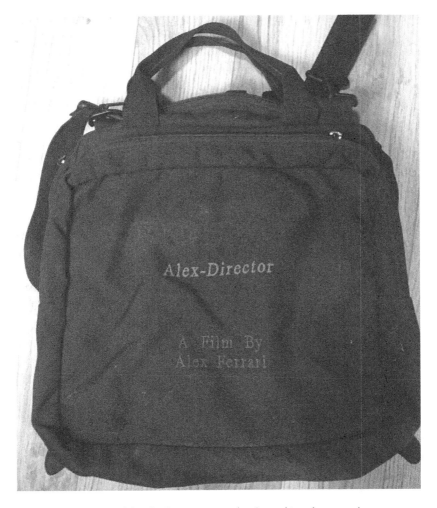

The director's bag that Jimmy gave me when I moved into the race track.

When I saw the front of it, I noticed that he'd had my name embroidered on the bag with the title *"You Gotta Go for It,* Directed by Alex Ferrari." I loved it. To this day I still have that director's bag and use it on all my big jobs.

This is how Jimmy pulled you deeper into his web. A few compliments here and a few gifts there. Promises he couldn't possibly keep, but you believed him at the time. It was the brilliance of his con.

He would invite people over to the offices to show them he was serious, that he really was making a movie. He would show them he had an office manager, accountant, and director working on his film.

People would believe he had to have something going on. If not, then why would these people be there with him? Jimmy must be paying them, right? This project had to be real. For weeks and months that's exactly what Jimmy would do; he'd parade people through the office and give them a tour of the racetrack, showing them where certain scenes were going to be shot.

Little did I know that this was how Jimmy was funding the project. Sometimes, the people would give Jimmy money to "invest" in the pre-production process, and sometimes they wouldn't. If the investor ever came back asking for money, Jimmy would do what Jimmy does: bark out threats in the manner that only he knew how to do. That would keep the poor investors at bay for months, if not for good. I have no idea how many thousands of dollars Jimmy blew through in those early months, but it was a ton.

THE WRITER

While I was rewriting the screenplay, I asked Jimmy multiple times if I could contact the original writer. He always said not to, that he was a bum and was not part of the project anymore. This was before IMDbPro, so I had no way of reaching out.

I asked Jimmy what had happened with the first writer.

"OK, kid, here's the story. Christian—the writer—my wife, and I had dinner one night with some potential investors and producers. The dinner is going well, then my wife excuses herself for a minute. Christian makes a joke about not getting paid for a rewrite on the script. He fucking sassed me in front of these investors. I get up from the table, look that mutha fucker in the eyes, and say, 'All right, you are going to get it, Christian.' This cocksucker starts to backpedal."

As you can imagine, the room was captivated by Jimmy's story.

"'I'm sorry, Jimmy, I didn't mean any disrespect.' I told him it was too late for that shit and that I would give him the first swing. This guy takes a wild fucking swing and misses. Then, I kicked him with my steel-tipped shoe. I always wear those shoes in case shit goes down, and I start to pound this prick on the floor. The restaurant clears out. The owners know who I am, so they leave me to it. When I'm done, I tell him he's done, and I start to leave. This guy grabs my feet and begs me not to leave until I forgive him.

"'Jimmy, I'm sorry for any disrespect. Please forgive me. Are we good?' This guy. Are we good? He wouldn't let me leave. He was crying, for God's sake. I told him we were good and to never sass me again. I grabbed my wife and left. With all of Christian's bullshit that night, the investors got scared away. Fucking guy."

Christian was a semiretired screenwriter. I guess he took this gig as an easy way to make a little extra cash, but there was nothing easy about it. For the next few months, Christian would call Jimmy looking for back money he was still owed. Jimmy would say, "How about the $15 million I've already poured into this project? Who's going to pay me back, Christian?"

There was no logic to what Jimmy said, but then again logic is something that was missing from his vocabulary.

Jimmy loved to call Christian up on speaker phone with the office listening, and threaten the poor guy. He had a heart condition, and Jimmy knew it. Christian begged Jimmy to stop threatening him. He said he was developing an ulcer because of this project and to please just pay him the money he was owed. Jimmy would lay down one more threat, hang up, and laugh so hard he'd tear up.

Christian's L.A. attorney even called Jimmy to request the money owed and to ask him to please stop threatening Christian because his client had a heart condition and was not doing well. Jimmy would laugh and hang up.

THE CANCER THAT TOOK OVER THE RACETRACK

We started to grow. We went from two small, dingy rooms on the first floor, to another main office on the second, and we would eventually take over the entire lounge on the third; the same lounge where we shot scenes for the sizzle reel.

It had been a few weeks since we fully moved in, and I had a sit-down with Jimmy. To this point, I hadn't been paid a cent for my time, the rewrite, or anything. When I moved into the office, I was promised $800 a week for pre-production. When I brought this to Jimmy's attention he said, "Sure, kid, no problem. I'm a man of my word."

He cut me a check for $800 right on the spot. This lasted for a few weeks; then Jimmy pulled me aside one day. "Look, kid, I can't keep fronting you money every week. I'll pay you any back pay once the money drops." He grabbed my shoulder and squeezed tightly. "I expect you to be loyal to me and the project, OK, kid? I don't want you turning colors on me. We understand each other?"

I nodded, and he left. This was the way it went for a while. Jimmy had some money, for sure, but he was too smart to put all of his cash into this dream of his. He'd borrow money from less than reputable lenders that demanded payment on-time.

He would get an influx of cash and then pay people a fraction of what they were owed. He would just keep stringing them along. I'd be paid for two weeks, then nothing for a month. During all that time Jimmy would just keep saying that the money was about to drop any day now.

Once the cash ran out, he'd find money from someone else to con. It wasn't easy keeping this carnival alive for almost a year. When money was low, the threats got bigger and louder. When money was in, he became nicer and calmer. It was like living with a bipolar grizzly.

WOULD YOU LIKE THAT SODA IN THE SHOT?

Product placement is something every major studio film has today. The earliest I can remember seeing product placement was when Elliot used Reese's Pieces to lure E.T. back to his house.

Can you believe M&M's passed on that product placement? They lost millions of dollars in free worldwide advertising. Companies either exchange product for exposure in the film or pay for the right to be seen in the final movie.

Generally, product placement is only available to major studio films, even back in the early 2000s. Independent films rarely got the opportunity to show products from larger brands in their projects.

Considering we were a small independent film about gangsters doing gangster things, there would be no chance that any brands would want to be associated with our film, right? You would think so, but as I soon discovered, you'd be wrong.

Enter Dave, our product placement guy. Imagine a sleazy used-car salesman who is tall, lanky, and always dressed in loud, tacky t-shirts, and you would have Dave. This guy saw a new con and was all over it.

Jimmy threw Francisco to Dave as an assistant, and it was a match made in heaven. Two used-car sales guys hustling product placement for an indie film that had no funding and no stars attached, but that didn't stop this dynamic duo.

I have to say, what Dave was able to do was pretty remarkable. Within two days of moving into the office, we received a huge shipment of computers from a *major* brand. Ten desktops and ten laptops just showed up. Overnight, the office was populated with thousands of dollars' worth of computers.

Jimmy didn't care much about the computers, because he hated technology and really hated computers. Anything that made him look weak or stupid he avoided like the plague. I was constantly helping him with basic email, printing scripts, and tech support.

All these computers were nice, but how was I going to place them in the film? I pulled Dave aside and said, "Dave, these are great, but this is a period film. These computers would be completely out of the time of the film. How am I supposed to product-place this brand's technology in a period film?"

Dave said, "No problem, we'll just stick their logo somewhere in the background. That's all we have to do contractually."

Wow, just wow. Next, Dave made a deal with a local luxury car dealership for the production to have a fleet of five brand-new 2002-model SUVs with GPS navigation. Having a GPS in your car back in 2001 was like witchcraft.

There was a catch. The deal was that we couldn't put more than three hundred miles on each car, so we'd have to swap out for new cars every few weeks. I brought up that point to Jimmy. "Jimmy, our film takes place in the sixties, seventies, and eighties, but these cars are 2002 models. Dave's product-placement deal is that the cars and the dealership's logo have to appear in the final film."

Jimmy's response was, "Don't worry, kid. We'll stick a car in the back of a scene somewhere. It'll be fine."

I know I was new to the world of product placement, but this was definitely not passing the sniff test. As days and weeks passed, more and more stuff kept coming in. At one point, I felt that Dave was using Jimmy's film production to get merchandise for himself. I could never prove that; it was just a feeling. A grifter grifting another grifter, it's poetic in a way.

I NEED TO GET OUT OF HERE

Months had passed, and I was owed a ton of back pay already. Jimmy was on the phone with agents and managers every day trying to get someone attached to this film. William Hurt and Robert Downey Jr. finally passed on the project when the budget never materialized.

There were only so many times I could rewrite the script and location scout around the racetrack. I was depressed, tired, and just beaten up.

I saw Francisco outside and pulled him aside. We sat down on an old bench overlooking the practice track. "Francisco, I have to leave this project. It's killing me. I'm in major debt. I keep charging up my credit cards just to stay afloat. I'm paying credit card bills with other credit cards. Jimmy owes me weeks of back pay. I just need to get out of here and get a job."

"You can't leave, man. Are you kidding? You're the director of Jimmy's film. If you leave, the entire production would fall apart, and guess who Jimmy would blame. You."

If I left the project, Francisco knew that not only would he lose his place in the production, but he would also be blamed for my leaving since he was the one who brought me into it in the first place.

Everything he was saying was for his sake, not mine. "Jimmy is still connected, man. You'd be risking your life if you left. Do you want to be looking over your shoulder for the rest of your life? And what do you think he'd do to me? I brought you into this project."

I told him I saw his point, but I just didn't know what to do.

"Just hang in there," he pleaded. "The money will be dropping any day now. This is a huge opportunity for you, brotha. Once you direct this film you can write your own ticket to Hollywood. Just don't mess it up."

I reluctantly agreed to stay on the project. Then Francisco said words that, to this day, I can't believe escaped his mouth. "So, we never discussed a finder's fee for me bringing you into the project and introducing you to Jimmy. I feel 10 percent is more than fair, don't you?"

Can you believe the balls on this guy? My life was crumbling around me and he's looking for a damn kickback. I just looked at him with utter disgust and walked away.

"Cool, cool. We'll talk about it later, then," he muttered.

THE OSCAR WINNER

One day Jimmy called me into his office and handed me the phone. He whispered the name of the Oscar-winning actor that was on the phone to me. I didn't believe him. Lo and behold, he was actually on the phone. I was a big fan of this actor and had seen all of his films.

I spoke to him for a few minutes. He was an extremely pleasant guy to talk to. He told me that he enjoyed the sizzle reel I directed and was very supportive of my directing the film. He also told me he looked forward to working with me on the project. Wait a minute, this Oscar-winning actor was going to be in my film? I was dazed and confused. I said my goodbyes and handed the phone back to Jimmy.

Jimmy then pulled out a letter of intent signed by the Oscar-winning actor. "It's on, kid. Didn't I tell you I could make it happen? You are going to be directing an Oscar-winning actor in your first fucking feature film. You are welcome."

You have to understand that to keep a project like this going like this for as long as Jimmy did was truly an art form. He knew that he couldn't, or wouldn't, pay me, but every so often I would get to talk to an Oscar winner, a big-time producer, or someone like that to keep the carrot he was dangling shiny and fresh. So I would continue believing the carrot was still there.

He did this with everyone. Once every few weeks or so, something new would happen that would keep hope alive for everyone to stay involved in the project, no matter how crazy it might get. The longer you stayed in, the harder it was to leave.

"Now that we have this, I can finally get the money to drop soon and we can get started."

I looked at the letter and it seemed legit. Later I discovered that any letter of intent is as worthless as the paper it's written on. All the letter represents is that the actor is aware of the project and may sign on if certain conditions are met (e.g., total budget, salary, credits, distribution guarantees, etc.). It doesn't mean they are officially attached to the project. It's basically worthless, but to the layman it looks super legit, and I was a layman for sure.

This letter would also work on "dumb money." Dumb money is uneducated or uninformed potential investors, people who just don't know how the film business works. If you wave around a letter signed by an Oscar winner, you'd be surprised just what you can get from green investors. And Jimmy did just that. Jimmy would pop out this letter and show it to anyone who walked into the office. I swear, I'm surprised it wasn't framed in his office so he could just point to it during meetings.

The letter gave Jimmy the ammo to continue the con. In his eyes, it legitimized him and the project, especially in the circles Jimmy ran in. With this letter he was able to keep the cash flowing, and the film production afloat, while he looked into other avenues for the full budget of the film.

THE BONDING COMPANY STRIKES AGAIN

The bonding company that had demanded I shoot a sizzle reel to prove I could direct the feature rose its ugly head once again. According to Jimmy, the company demanded he bring on a "more credible" feature film director as a consultant to secure the big stars needed to lock up the budget for the film. Also, the budget had to drop from $20 million to $8 million with me attached as the director.

I had never spoken to this director or had any communication with him. All I had was a signed letter stating that he vouched for me as the director and would be available to come in and take over if something went wrong. Gotta tell you, that was a real morale booster. The director in question had done a couple of films back in the '80s—you would know them if I named them—but he hadn't made anything in over fifteen years.

Jimmy kept reminding me, almost daily, that he was putting himself out there for me, that he still believed in me, and that he would fight to keep me on this film. He also told me that my salary for directing the film, which was already insultingly low for a film of this size, had to be dropped by half and I would have to defer the rest. What was I supposed to say? No, I won't do that, and try to speak to my agent? Oh, wait, my agent was the gangster producer of the film. Talk about a conflict of interest.

Over time, I came to realize that Jimmy never spoke to a bonding company. All of these demands were from him. That last-minute additional scene for the sizzle reel, was Jimmy just wanting another scene.

He used the bonding company as a legitimate excuse to make me jump through hoops, or make me believe he had my back. I didn't realize this until years later. It's tough to see things clearly when you are in the middle of the storm.

CASTING THE LOCALS

Billy, our casting director, had a long history with Jimmy. He'd been on this project for years, working for free. Since he was a small-time local casting director, Jimmy used him the same way he used me, by dangling that golden Hollywood carrot.

Jimmy would send out packages to actors in Los Angeles weekly. Billy would pack a VHS copy of the sizzle reel, a script, and a custom offer letter to each actor or producer. One day as I was walking the halls, I heard Jimmy screaming at the top of his lungs. I peeked into his office and saw Jimmy holding Billy against the wall.

Apparently, Billy had sent an offer letter to an actor with another actor's name on it. The actor's agent called Jimmy and ripped into him. As you can imagine, that didn't go well. Poor Billy was scared for his life. Jimmy was spouting threats left and right. He was almost foaming at the mouth. The room was still.

Once Jimmy let him go and Billy's feet touched the floor, he took off running and was nowhere to be found for weeks. He literally went into hiding, thinking Jimmy was going to kill him. Eventually, Billy came back after Jimmy cooled off and forgave him. Just another day in paradise.

Since I had nothing to do all day, I asked Jimmy if we could start casting some of the smaller roles in the film locally. He loved the idea. Billy started to send me headshots for the smaller roles.

One morning, walking into the racetrack, I saw a line of half-naked women standing by the office. Billy set up a casting call without telling me. Jimmy wanted to have a casting of a "key scene" in the film—the strip club sequence. *Of course he does*, I said to myself. We went to the first floor where there was a large room painted an institutional yellow from the floor to the ceiling.

"Finally, the kid got here." You could hear Jimmy's impatience coming through. "Now we can get started."

"What's going on, Jimmy?"

"We are casting the strip club scene. Today we make you a man, kid."

The gang cracked up. Jimmy, Richard, Billy, and a few of his wise-guy friends sat behind a table and Jimmy invited girl after girl, all dressed in character, to come in and show us their portfolios, which consisted of nude shots of themselves. There is nothing more uncomfortable than meeting someone for the first time and looking at a picture of her naked.

At that moment in my life, I had been with a steady girlfriend for some time. I wasn't comfortable, to say the least. I'd never cast for roles like this.

Sometimes Jimmy would just tell the girls straight to their faces that they were too fat or just not that good-looking, and the gang would laugh at them. I had no idea what to do. This couldn't be the way scenes like this are cast.

One girl found out I was the director and pulled me aside. She looked me straight in the eyes and told me, "I'd do anything to get a part in this film . . . *anything.*"

I turned into that shy high school guy who had no idea how to speak to women.

"I think you broke him, honey," Jimmy told the girl.

She smiled and said, "My contact info is on the back of my head-shot."

The peanut gallery started to laugh hysterically. She kept smiling.

She kissed me on the cheek and walked out. Jimmy and the boys saw this and busted out laughing. They came over to congratulate me as if I had won something. I was so embarrassed I just walked out.

"Where you going, kid?" asked Jimmy as I was walking out the door.

"I need to make a call," I called over my shoulder.

"Is that what you kids call it these days, 'making a call'?"

Again the room burst into laughter. I quickly walked out of the room as the auditions continued, called my then-girlfriend, and told her everything. I did nothing wrong, but felt really guilty for some reason.

I was a professional who took what I did very seriously, and this was unprofessional. I would never treat any actor or actress like that, but I felt powerless. I couldn't stand up for myself, let alone for someone else. There are ways to cast a scene like this, and this was not one of them. I didn't go back in the room for the rest of that "casting session."

THE DENTIST

Jimmy invited me to go out to lunch with a potential investor in the film. The guy was literally a dentist; I'm not joking. I felt like Johnny Depp in *Ed Wood* hustling dentists for money. As we dined at this extremely upscale restaurant, Jimmy weaved this amazing tale about how he had been trying to make this film for fifteen years and how he'd flown out to Hollywood many times. He said he met huge stars, agents, and producers, and that he was an expert on how to play the Hollywood game.

Jimmy told a story about when he was eating at Spago's in Beverly Hills and saw a young Mark Wahlberg. Mark was post–*Boogie Nights* and coming up. Jimmy loved him. He sent a bottle of the most expensive wine in the place to Mark's table. Mark came over to thank him for the gesture, and he actually recognized Jimmy. Mark mentioned that he was doing research for a film about the mob, and that Jimmy's name came up during his research. Mark turned into a fan boy and sat down at the table.

This dentist was in awe of Jimmy; like I said before, he could tell a story like no other.

Jimmy pulled me aside before the bill came and said, "Look, kid, I can't keep paying for all these meals. This is your shot, so pay the bill."

I was shocked and said, "Jimmy I don't have that kind of cash."

Jimmy didn't care. He said, "Kid, I don't care what you have to do, just handle it. This is your dream, not mine, so pay the check. I'll leave the tip."

And with that, I busted out my credit card and charged it up. As my grandfather always said, what's another stripe on the tiger? As we all started to leave the table, Jimmy pulled out a wad of cash, held together with a rubber band, and plopped down one hundred dollars as a tip to impress the dentist. It worked. That dentist funded the production for a few weeks.

Jimmy would walk around with a wad full of cash but rarely used it. He would twist the arms of others to pay so that he would look like a big shot. The wad of cash was a prop in the theater of Jimmy. He loved playing the part of a gangster. He loved the respect it got him. He loved being the center of attention. He loved controlling people. Why wouldn't he want to be in Hollywood?

THE COMMERCIAL

I got a call one morning from the production company that represents me as a commercial- and music-video director. Things had been quiet for a while, so this phone call was well-received.

My rep was calling to offer me a local series of commercials. The pay was respectable, and man, did I need the money. Jimmy was already months behind on my pay, and I was using credit cards to pay my mortgage.

They sent me the storyboards, and I really liked what I saw. Finally, something without mobsters in it. The production would be simple: two days of prep, one day of shooting, and a week of post-production. We'd shoot on film and be out of there within two weeks.

"I know you are in the middle of your big feature film, but I know you are in soft prep," said the rep. "So, if you can pull yourself away for a couple of weeks, you can make some quick cash."

"Sounds good to me. Let me pass it by my producer, but I think it'll be fine."

As I said those words, I got really nervous. Would Jimmy let me go to shoot this? I needed the money bad. I was literally running on fumes.

The next day, I walked into Jimmy's office and sat down at his desk. He was joking around with Sid and Sam. "What can I do for you, kid?"

"Hey, Jimmy. Listen, the production company that reps me for commercials just offered me a quick gig."

His demeanor changed.

"Are you turning colors on me, kid?"

"No, Jimmy, of course not. It's just for a couple of weeks, and I can make some quick cash. This will keep me afloat for a bit until the financing drops for the film."

Jimmy thought to himself for a minute. If he let me go shoot this commercial and actually get paid, that would keep me happy and, in his mind, I would owe him.

"OK, kid, go and shoot your commercial. We'll be here slaving away trying to get this movie made while you are off making tons of cash."

"Trust me, it's not tons of cash, but it'll keep my skills sharp."

"Alright, but you owe me one."

"Thanks, Jimmy. Let me know if anything happens while I'm gone."

And with that, I was free for the time being. I went into production the following week. I booked Hugo, the director of photography from the sizzle reel, as my cinematographer and got a bunch of the crew from the trailer on the job.

I would tell anyone who would listen that I was directing a huge Hollywood feature with big stars attached. It was strange. I wanted to get away from Jimmy and his madness, but I loved being a part of making a feature film. I really didn't know which way to go.

To be honest, I was a tough person to be around in those days. Without Jimmy to flatten my ego a bit, I was unleashed. Let's be honest, I was a douche.

At one point, my arrogance was getting so bad that the client who was paying me called my rep and said, "Listen, I hired this guy to direct my commercials. I don't give a shit about who is in his fucking feature film. When I call, I expect him to pick up and not push me off because he's on the line with a fucking movie star."

My rep was so embarrassed. I was fucking up left and right. Not the directing part, but everything else. I was doing my job, but I was just hard to handle.

The production company called me on-set and had a come-to-Jesus talk with me. They explained everything and told me to calm the fuck down. There was a lot of money at stake here. I heard everything loud and clear. I eventually got on the right track and went back to work.

The commercial shoot went well after that. The client was super happy with the final product, and the production company was singing my praises. Plus, I got a much-needed check.

It was a bittersweet experience. I had an opportunity to do what I loved to do and get paid for it. The gig gave me a moment of freedom from my current prison. I hadn't heard from Jimmy in two weeks, but I'd be going back to my cage soon.

When I showed up at the racetrack the next day, I was treated to a wall of attitude from Jimmy, Sid, and Sam. "Oh, His Highness is back," said Jimmy. "Did you shoot your little commercial? I'm sorry you have to come back to the ghetto of making a feature fucking film."

"Jimmy, of course I'm happy to be back. I missed you guys."

No, I didn't.

"Well, if you are done directing bullshit commercials and want to get back to working on making a real film, then let me know. 'Cause if not, I have ten directors on the line just dying to get on this show. Some of whom are Oscar nominees."

Was this my out? Could I just walk away from this hell? I was about to say something like, *I'll be happy to step aside if that'll help the film,* but before I could get two words out Jimmy burst out laughing. "I'm just kidding, kid. You know you're my guy. Hope you enjoyed your mini vacation. Now get back to fucking work and make this film happen."

That sucked the energy right out of me. I went back to my day-to-day existence of waiting for money to drop while listening to Jimmy yell and threaten people on the phone or in-person. Little did I know that this crazy train was about to take a drastic turn and give me an experience that would change me forever.

CHAPTER 8

Let's Go to Hollyweird

After months of sending out packages we finally started getting bites from Hollywood. Jimmy pulled me into his office and told me, "Kid, it's time. We're going to Hollywood, you up for it?"

I was so excited. I would finally be out of the prison that was the racetrack. I'd never been to Hollywood before. California was a dream-like place I had only seen in the movies. This was going to be amazing.

"I've got a bunch of meetings set up, and they all want to meet you. Pack nice so you don't embarrass me," Jimmy cautioned.

Jimmy said he would take care of everything, and to his credit, he did. I never paid for anything when I traveled with him. At the racetrack we were starving, but when we traveled it was first-class accommodations all the way. There was just one problem: Jimmy was scared to death of flying.

Poor Richard had to spend hours looking for a flight from the New Orleans International Airport to Los Angeles, and the plane needed to be an Airbus 340; the largest commercial airliner of its day.

It didn't matter what it cost; Jimmy felt he was safer in a larger airplane. He told me he believed "wicked people" shouldn't fly. I guess for someone who always wanted to be in-control, flying must have been a nightmare.

I had never traveled with Jimmy before, and trust me, it was an adventure. I met him at the airport, and when he came around the corner, I couldn't believe what I was seeing.

He was wearing a solid-gold tracksuit, white tank top, gold chains, a leather coat, and, to top it all off, a black fedora with a huge feather in it. I shit you not.

As stereotypical as that might sound, it was true. He would never dress like that in the office. It was just when he traveled. As we walked through the airport, all we got were confused stares from people. I mean, he looked ridiculous, but man, Jimmy thought he was stylish.

Jimmy always took something to knock him out for flights. This time it was taking a bit longer for the pill to kick in. We were in the air, and he was gripping the chair so tightly that his knuckles were turning white.

"Jimmy, is that smoke coming from the wing?" I asked, enjoying his discomfort for a change.

"Shut up, kid!" he snarled.

Oddly enough, this was the only place in the world where I felt I had power over Jimmy, and I had fun with him.

"Seriously, Jimmy, I think I saw the wing rattle a bit. Do you think something is loose?"

"Shut the fuck up, kid."

Once the Dramamine kicked in Jimmy was out. I sat there in my First Class seat, excited beyond words. I was flying to Hollywood to meet producers, actors, agents, and God knows who else. Trips like this were why it was so hard to leave this situation. I don't know how Jimmy did this, but I honestly didn't care at the time. I was just along for the ride.

WELCOME TO HOLLYWOOD

We stayed at the Sofitel Los Angeles in Beverly Hills, across the street from the Beverly Center; a huge indoor mall. I was raised in New York and remembered life in the big city, but Los Angeles was different. Everyone seemed beautiful, as if I were in a world of models. I felt like Axel Foley walking around in *Beverly Hills Cop* for the first time. It was a wonderland.

Jimmy had set up a meeting that night at the world-famous Chateau Marmont with an actor who was interested in being in the film, but he wouldn't tell me his name. We drove up in a cab to this Hollywood castle. As I walked in, I saw celebrity after celebrity having drinks, talking, and laughing with all sorts of beautiful people. It seemed otherworldly to me. All the furniture was antique, and the lighting was warm, but dimmed, to hide the faces of the celebrities in the room.

I was in a daze. We walked to the back of the lounge area and sat in these beautifully ornate chairs. The waiter came over and asked for our order. Jimmy asked for gin, and I had a glass of water. I don't drink. I'm boring that way. We sat around waiting for the actor to show up, soaking in the room.

"Not bad, right?" Jimmy asked

"This is pretty cool, Jimmy."

Jimmy nudged me. "Look, this actor is coming with his agent, and he wants to give you the smell test, so be prepared to answer questions about yourself and the project."

"Got it."

"Don't embarrass me, kid."

Just then *the actor* walks up with his agent. I was starstruck. I grew up watching this guy in huge blockbuster films, and some were my favorite films of all time. We'll call the actor "T-Rex." T-Rex introduced himself to me and sat down with his agent in-tow.

I soon realized that T-Rex was fascinated with Jimmy. He would be playing Jimmy in the film, after all. He kept asking Jimmy questions about his days as a gangster, and of course, Jimmy didn't disappoint.

He told story after story while T-Rex sat there like a child listening to a bedtime story.

As the meeting went on, the agent asked about the film's financing and mentioned that rumor around Hollywood was that the money was coming from the mob, which he was oddly perfectly OK with. Jimmy played the game and said he couldn't tell them where the money was coming from, but that he had it. The agent asked for a huge payday for T-Rex, and Jimmy didn't blink.

"If T-Rex will be in my film, we can make that happen."

You see, if T-Rex signed on to the film, getting the money for the budget would become much easier.

Now that it was settled, everyone's attention focused on me. Who was this unknown director? After speaking to me for a while, T-Rex said he had no problem with me directing him.

For being such a huge movie star, I have to say that, to this day, T-rex is one of the kindest people I've ever met in Hollywood. You could tell he was a movie star, because when he walked into the room he sucked the energy right out of it. It was all about him, and not in a bad way—his presence demanded attention. I'd never experienced that before.

The meeting came to an end. When the bill came Jimmy grabbed the check and pulled out that wad of hundred-dollar bills. T-Rex and his agent were shocked and mumbled to themselves in glee. They were hanging out with a real mobster.

We all got up from the table and said our goodbyes. T-Rex was nothing but flattering to me as he shook my hand, but then the agent pulled me aside, away from earshot of Jimmy, and asked me if I could handle the film, because I wouldn't have Jimmy to protect me on the set. He said, "You'd be directing an Oscar nominee. This isn't commercials; this is the real fucking deal."

My ignorance of what was happening was to my benefit. I had no idea who this guy was, so I snapped back at him, "Listen, I've been busting my ass for this opportunity for years, so if I say I can do something, that's what I mean. I'll make your client look amazing. Don't worry."

"That's all I wanted to hear," said the agent. He was testing me to see what I would do. I had no idea. This wouldn't be the first or the last time I would be tested by actors, producers, or agents.

The agent firmly shook my hand and left with T-Rex. After Jimmy and I sat back down, he asked me if I knew who the agent was, and I told him no. I came to find out that I had just puffed up my chest to a partner in arguably one of the largest talent agencies in Hollywood. I nearly shit myself. I knew his name; hell, I'd even read his book about how he built his agency. Jimmy didn't want to tell me so I wouldn't get nervous. I'm glad he didn't. Ignorance was bliss.

Since I'd already had my first big Hollywood meeting on my first night in Los Angeles, I couldn't wait to see what the next day had to offer.

THE PRODUCERS

The next day we went to Spago's for lunch. When I walked in all I could see were wall-to-wall celebrities, directors, and producers. Not one table I walked past wasn't talking business. Jimmy said we were meeting some young up-and-coming producers who were hungry and loved the script and trailer I shot.

Up walked two well-dressed guys, both wearing sports coats, jeans, and expensive cowboy boots. This must've been the L.A. uniform for producers and directors, because everyone in the restaurant was dressed the same.

Jimmy introduced Bobby and Shane to me. These guys were in the middle of post-production on a big film over at Miramax. They were players. Up until then I had only met wannabes.

They gushed over Jimmy, praising the script and trailer. They loved the story and wanted to see how they could help Jimmy get the film made. Jimmy, of course, loved the attention. He told a few stories about how Hollywood had been screwing him for fifteen years and how he was married to the streets. The boys ate it up.

Shane asked Jimmy if he had ever been in touch with the producers of *The Sopranos*, and Jimmy told him he'd met those guys a while ago, but he couldn't stand the creator. He said, "I told that cocksucker that if I ever saw even a little of my story on his fuckin' show, I'd come after him and straighten him out for good. What gangster would be talking to a shrink? That's some Hollywood bullshit."

Shane and Bobby smiled and gave a nervous laugh. I asked Bobby straight up, "How are you going to handle the whole I'm-a-first-time-director issue? We've been getting pushback about having me attached to the film."

Bobby said, "You are my director, and it's my job as the producer to go out and fight for you and your vision. If they bust my balls on this picture, then I'll bust their balls on the next one. I'll make sure you are on set doing what you do."

This was the best answer to that question I had ever heard. I was actually talking to a real producer for once in my life. Bobby and Shane said they would work long-distance from L.A. and try to gather the financing as well as help with casting. Jimmy was excited to have some producers with real credits finally on the film.

The boys got up and went to their next meeting. I started to get up to leave, but Jimmy pulled me back. "We are meeting someone else. Sit down, kid."

A few minutes later this kind of slimy guy walked up to the table. His name was Bruce. Apparently, Bruce heard about the project and reached out to Jimmy to see what he could do. After hearing him speak for five minutes, I realized he was the L.A. version of Francisco, a bottom-feeder trying to jump on the ship before it took off.

He had no money, but he did have one thing to offer: a connection to a *huge* film producer—Richard Bigtime. My eyes lit up. Jimmy didn't know who he was until I told him the name of his latest $800 million hit film. Jimmy woke up after that.

Bruce straight up told Jimmy that if he made this meeting happen and something came from it, he wanted a finder's fee of $25,000. Jimmy happily agreed. I was sure, even if Jimmy was having issues paying me $800 a week, he'd have no problem paying the $25K to this guy. Bruce gave us Richard's cell number and told Jimmy to call him in the morning to let him know how the meeting went.

Later, Jimmy called Richard and did what Jimmy did so well: he talked his way into a meeting. Richard invited us to his penthouse in Brentwood. We were going up to see the wizard.

MEETING THE WIZARD

The taxi dropped us off in front of a stunning apartment building. We walked into the cavernous lobby with modern art hanging on the walls. A doorman sat in front of this huge desk.

"We are here to see Richard Bigtime," Jimmy told the doorman.

"Of course, Mr. Bigtime is expecting you," and he ushered us into a private elevator, swiped a card, and pushed a button, sending us directly to Mr. Bigtime's floor, where the doors opened directly into Richard's apartment taking up the entire floor.

I swear I felt like I was in a movie. The entire experience was surreal. We were greeted by Richard's assistant, Remy, who said, "Mr. Bigtime will be with you in a moment. Please have a seat in the living room." He reminded me of Lloyd from HBO's *Entourage*.

The apartment was out of this world. All the exterior walls were made of glass, from the floor to the ceiling. The views of Los Angeles were breathtaking. Jimmy was playing it cool, but I could tell he was impressed.

We sat down and waited for Richard. Movie posters of all his films were framed throughout the house. Movie after movie I grew up watching. Then Richard made his entrance. He introduced himself and thanked us both for coming by. He turned to Jimmy and said, "I hear from Bruce that you have an amazing project."

Jimmy went into the pitch, telling his stories, what he had gone through to get to this point, and how he had been abused by Hollywood over the past fifteen years. Then he asked Richard if he had seen the trailer that I directed for the film. Richard said he had not, but if we had a copy with us, we could watch it in his screening room.

Jimmy handed him a VHS copy. We walked over to his screening room on the other side of the apartment. When I walked in all I could see were memorabilia, posters, framed box-office numbers from *Variety* and *The Hollywood Reporter* of that $800 million hit-film he produced. I felt like I was in *True Romance* when Christian Slater met the big-time film producer at the end of the film.

Richard popped the VHS in, and we all watched it on this huge projector screen. Honestly, the trailer had never looked or sounded better. After it was over Richard turned to me and shook my hand. "Well done, young man. This shows me that you are a director with vision. Seriously, nice job."

Not wanting to be left out, Jimmy asked, "Can I pick a winner or what, Richard?"

Did Richard Bigtime just congratulate me on a trailer I directed? This guy works with the biggest directors in the business. I barely gathered up enough air to say thank you.

We walked back to his living room and started talking shop. Richard and I hit it off right away and talked about films, filmmaking, and everything movies for almost two hours. It was amazing. I told him about my time working at a video store and how I would watch his films again and again. Jimmy sat there like a bump on a log. He couldn't keep up with us.

Richard turned to Jimmy and said, "I think Mel and Robert would be perfect for this film."

I wanted to clarify what he meant, so I asked him if he was talking about Mel Gibson and Robert Downey Jr., and he said that Mel had been looking to do another film with Robert for years, ever since *Air America*, and he thought they'd love this project. He said he was seeing Mel the following day on the set of M. Night's new film and he'd pitch my film to him and let us know what happened.

I didn't say a word. I waited to see what Jimmy would say. He didn't disappoint. "Richard, we were talking to Robert a few months ago, but we couldn't lock him in."

Richard smiled. "That's my job, Jimmy. Bobby is a personal friend. I'll reach out to him tomorrow."

This was one of those rare times when Jimmy couldn't contain his genuine excitement. Richard turned to me and said, "You have a good script here." Then he turned to Jimmy. "Don't let go of this guy; he's going to be a big-time director one day, so you'd better be nice to him now while we can all still afford him."

We laughed, and I thanked Richard for his kind words. But still, I had my worries, so I had to ask, "Richard, why would an Academy Award–winning director like Mel Gibson work with a first-time director?"

"Don't worry, Alex. Mel loves filmmakers; he'll be there on set with you every day, backing you up. He's done it before."

I was happy but nervous at the possibility of working with such an experienced actor and director. I smiled and thanked Richard for his time. We said our goodbyes and were on our way. When we got in the elevator and the doors closed, we were both quiet for a second; then Jimmy smacked me on the back.

"Did I deliver or what, kid? Mel fucking Gibson. We'll be off and running in no time. You just keep prepping the film."

I agreed and smiled all the way back down to the street. It was one hell of a way to finish my first trip to Los Angeles. *Is this the way things happen in L.A.? Do doors open this easily?* It all seemed too good to be true. It would be interesting to see what happens back at the racetrack.

CHAPTER 9

Building the Motley Crew

Jimmy was really jazzed up from our trip. After fifteen years of hustling this project, he was finally moving into high gear. When he told the gang at the office about Mr. Bigshot and how he was so enthusiastic about making this film, you could feel the energy change. People really thought we were on our way to making this thing.

Jimmy pulled me into the office and asked me, "Kid, what do you need to really start prepping this movie?"

"I need crew, specifically department heads. Cinematographer, 1st assistant director, production designer, etc."

"Done. I want to show people we are serious and that we are going to make this movie. I'll start making some calls."

I was too excited for words. After months of just sitting around this old, rundown racetrack I was going to actually start prepping this film with a crew.

Jimmy talked to the building manager and hustled his way into a few more rooms in the track. The main office moved upstairs, and we took over an entire cigar lounge on the third floor. This was going to be our main production office.

The lounge was blood-red with flower designs throughout. Old mahogany dripped from the walls. The ceiling was covered in a gold, reflective material. It wasn't like any production office I'd ever seen before, but it was mine.

At the end of the lounge, Jimmy built me a makeshift office with a door so I could have some privacy. This was looking like a production office. Other than the fact that it was in a closed-down cigar lounge at a racetrack, it was legit. Now it was time to find some crew and fill it up.

Like everything in this project, Jimmy wanted crew with cache, with real Hollywood credits. Finding good-quality local department heads with feature-film credits would be tough. I told Jimmy to put the word out and try to find a local production designer, but we should get a 1st AD and cinematographer from L.A.

I interviewed probably twenty production designers that week, but I settled on a guy with the best presentation. Jerry had amazing film credits. Practically every major motion picture that came to the area would call Jerry. It's always better to hire production designers locally, especially on low-budget films, because they know how to source materials, crew, sets, etc., more affordably.

Once we had Jerry on-board, he had Jimmy build a "look wall" in the middle of our production office. He could then start putting together a color representation of the entire film, scene by scene. We'd staple reference photos of looks, cars, set plans, locations, characters, actor headshots, and colors.

This gave you an overall feeling for how the film was going to look. Jimmy loved that idea. Anything that could make it look like we were legit, he was all about it. Jerry and I wouldn't become best friends, or friends at all—hell, I never spoke to him again after the project—but he was professional and giving of his time. He taught me about color science, set construction, and how to pick locations properly, among other things.

MEETING A LEGEND

Next up was the 1st assistant director. Jimmy made friends with a legendary 1st AD in his travels to Hollywood over the years; his name was Frank.

Frank worked on some of the biggest Hollywood blockbusters of the '70s, '80s, and '90s, working with directors like David Fincher, Martin Scorsese, John Badham, Lawrence Kasdan, and many more. To a kid who had only experienced Hollywood through a video store and LaserDisc commentaries, I was in awe.

Jimmy called Frank up and told him, "It's time, Frank. We're making the movie." He was on the next plane from L.A.

When I met Frank for the first time, I was taken by how generous he was to me. He started to take me through the process of breaking down the film. I'd directed tons of commercials, but this was different. Breaking down a feature film was a science and an art.

Frank was old-school. Even though he did have a laptop, he still preferred to schedule the film in strips and a board. Each scene was broken down into one strip, and we would move these strips around by day. The schedule was determined by seeing how many scenes could be shot in any one day. It was truly an art. Frank would know how many hours it would take to shoot a certain kind of scene and allot the proper time.

The schedule was a living creature that was always changing depending on a myriad of variables: locations, actors' schedules, budget, camera, etc. Frank and I would spend days working out the schedule, and I loved every minute of it. It was like having Yoda teach you the force.

Frank told me a story about when Jimmy was visiting him in Los Angeles at the backlot of Sony. Frank's office was down the hall from legendary producer Jerry Bruckheimer. He and a young director by the name of Michael Bay were working on a film called *Bad Boys*.

Jimmy walked into the building dressed like an extra from *A Bronx Tale*, and everyone stopped in their tracks. Michael Bay was editing with Jerry, and they both popped their heads out of the door to see Jimmy walk down to Frank's office. Later, Jerry would ask Frank if he was the real deal. I don't know why Hollywood people are so fascinated by gangsters, but they are. Jimmy knew this and played it up. He loved the attention.

More on my adventures with Frank later. We still had a cinematographer to hire.

SUPERHERO CINEMATOGRAPHER

I had a great time working with Hugo on the trailer, but Jimmy wanted a cinematographer with more credits. After watching countless demo reels Jimmy settled on a guy whose big claim to fame was being the second-unit cinematographer on a big Hollywood comic-book film.

He hired him without asking me. Jimmy thought he knew best in this area because he'd been studying Hollywood for fifteen years; he thought he was an expert. After watching his demo, I was not very impressed. I told Jimmy that this guy wasn't that great and didn't have the credits he was looking for. Jimmy started to yell at the top of his lungs, "Don't question my decisions. I'll bust your skull wide open and straighten you out for good. Do you understand? Do you fuckin' understand?"

The vibration of his voice shook the pencils on his desk. You really never knew when Jimmy was going to go off that way. Sometimes I could see the signs, but other times, like then, I had no idea. It was like playing Russian roulette every day.

I never saw Jimmy throw a punch. His technique was to use his perceived mobbish history and bark as loud as he could so he wouldn't have to throw that punch. I nodded and walked away.

"Don't forget who's the captain of this ship." But he knew I was right, and kept looking even though the cinematographer he hired was already prepping to come.

The next day, Jimmy called me into his office, and I caught him watching a demo reel. I saw a few movies I recognized. The lighting and camera work were stellar, so I asked, "Who's this?"

He quickly turned off the television and said, "A new cinematographer I'm scouting. I think he'll be a better match for you. Now, since you are the director of this film, call up that other DP and fire him."

"What?" I was shocked.

Jimmy looked annoyed with me, as if I was to blame for hiring the DP he had hired. "If you want this new guy, handle your business and fire the other guy."

Amazing. I didn't hire this poor guy, but I had to fire him. Under it all, Jimmy was a coward. Having a kid do his dirty work was a new level of crappy. I called the poor cinematographer, and as you can imagine, the man was livid. He had turned down three other films because Jimmy booked him. He slammed the phone down and the line went dead.

ENTER THE BORIS

After having to fire a cinematographer I didn't hire, Jimmy gave me a VHS demo reel of the new DP he liked. I popped it into the deck and started to watch. The images were beautiful. I recognized a bunch of the work on the demo reel. Big stars. Large productions. But the most stunning visuals came from the images I didn't recognize, shots from foreign films in eastern Europe.

At the end of the demo his name came up, Boris. I was blown away. I ran back into Jimmy's office and told him I had to work with this cinematographer. "I told you, kid. Don't question me again. I'll check him out and let you know what I come up with."

Jimmy got on the phone with Boris's agent to discuss the film. The agent told Jimmy that Boris was on the east coast finishing up a job and wanted to read the script before he committed to the gig. Jimmy was so impressed that Boris wanted to read the script first that he hired him on the spot. The agent was taken aback, but she agreed.

The agent called Boris, who was packing his bags to go back home to Los Angeles, and told him that if he wanted the job, it was his. Boris asked why he had been hired so fast, and the agent said, "Because you asked to read the script." Boris couldn't believe it, but said OK and read the script I'd rewritten. He loved it and got on a plane to come start pre-production.

I went to meet Boris at his hotel. When I got to the lobby, I saw this massive guy, must've been six and a half feet tall. I walked over to him and asked, "Are you Boris?"

Boris smiled, gave me a firm handshake, and said, "My friend, it's great to meet you." I loved him right away. I'd never met anyone from Europe before. His accent was a bit strong. Think a watered-down Borat. We started chatting about the film, what my vision was for the movie, and other geeky camera stuff. We became fast friends.

Jimmy walked up and said, "Boris, I hear good things about you."

Boris thanked him for the opportunity and told him he loved the story. We all sat down and started talking about the script. Jimmy admitted that he didn't have a specific vision for the film and said, "It's you and the kid's job to make me look good."

But he did have one demand from Boris. "Boris, I need one thing from you. We have to shoot my film on Panavision cameras."

Boris looked surprised and asked, "Panavision is a great camera, but why does it have to be Panavision?"

"Because every big Hollywood film I've ever seen has that Panavision logo in the credits. I want that logo in my credits," Jimmy told him.

Boris was stunned. He'd never heard a producer demand the use of a certain camera because he liked the logo, and he told him, "Jimmy, based on the budget you faxed me, I don't think we can afford a Panavision camera package."

Jimmy, once again acting like the big shot, said, "Don't you worry. If you need a bit more money for Panavision, I'll make it happen. Also, I already hired your gaffer, key grip, and camera assistant."

This didn't go over well with Boris. "Jimmy, I usually hire my own crew."

"Don't worry, Boris, I vouch for them. They are good guys. You'll be happy, trust me."

Boris reluctantly nodded his head. Jimmy got up to get the car. We were all going out to dinner. Once Jimmy left, Boris turned to me. "Is Jimmy serious, or is he just pulling the leg?"

"It's 'pulling my leg' and no, he's not. I'll fill you in later," I told him.

At that moment Boris was questioning his decision to come to Hotel Jimmy. He had no idea.

THE FOOTBALL COACH

Next up was Jimmy's location manager, Chip, who had been with him on this odyssey for ten years, helping when he could. He also helped us out big time on the sizzle reel. Chip was a professional location manager and worked on huge features around the world. He was a very large man, always dressed like a high school football coach. He rocked a *Magnum P.I.* mustache as well.

I loved Chip right away. His energy was infectious. He was always positive and had an amazing outlook on things no matter how grim the situation. One funny thing about Chip was that he was the kindest conservative you would ever meet. He had some very interesting views on life. I came over to his apartment one day to go over some location photos. He loved guns, I mean *loved* them. He opened up this huge vault in his living room. As the door swung open all you could see was grey and black metal. Guns and rifles filled the vault from top to bottom.

"Chip, why so many guns?"

"It's just a hobby. You start with one and it just balloons from there."

Chip would later tell me his views about politics, how being a conservative in Hollywood was tough, and his views on mating with the opposite sex. The crazy thing about all of his views was that he was so pleasant and funny as he told me. Just amazing. Chip always cracked me up, but he was also very good at his job.

He taught me how to location scout, how to always have cash in the pocket to pay off that neighbor who decides to cut the lawn in the middle of your shot, and how to provide location owners with a sanitized script. He also taught me that it was better to ask for forgiveness and get my shot than to ask for permission and lose a scene.

He would also end almost every sentence with "It'll be *fantastic!*" It's fair to say that I really liked Chip.

My crew was coming together. Now we could get to work and start prepping this film, if Jimmy didn't get in the way.

CHAPTER 10

What Are We, Barbarians?

Once the crew was in place, we began to put this film together. Every day for me was like going to film school. Every department would sit me down and educate me on what they were doing. A typical day would consist of walking down that long hall to the end, where I'd walk into our makeshift production office. I'd settle in, have a quick production meeting, and see what would be happening that day.

Considering we didn't have a start date for principal photography, it was like we were training for a heavyweight title fight but had no idea when that fight would be. The team and I would just always have to be in a state of readiness. This was *not* how you make a movie.

During one of those early-morning production meetings Boris asked for a cup of coffee. We told him there was none. "What are we, barbarians? Permission to leave, my captain. I'll be back in a couple of hours."

"Sure, Boris. Where are you going?"

"It'll be a surprise, my friend," he said and left. I continued the meeting with the other department heads. I went over to Frank to figure out how the hell we were going to schedule this movie. Frank was old school. He did use a computer, like I said before, but he lived and died by the scheduling strip.

We would spend hours breaking down the film, moving scenes back and forth, trying to make something work. I figured out that scheduling a film was like a fluid dance. You would move one way and then something would stop you and you would have to move another way. Obstacles like actors' schedules, the sun, the time of day, the location schedule, action sequences, etc. We even had a yearly turtle migration that would have stopped us from shooting a crucial scene in the bayou. So many logistics to deal with, and Frank handled it like a pro. He really taught me how to roll with the punches.

As promised, an hour later Boris walked back into the office with a huge cappuccino maker under his arm. The entire office erupted in applause.

"We are not savages, my friend. We will have cappuccino!"

Apparently, a cappuccino to Boris was like air. He set up the machine and started to make coffee for everyone. This would be his job for the remainder of the shoot. Every morning you'd find Boris at the cappuccino machine making coffee for everyone. I even brought in some of my Cuban coffee for Boris to try. He fell in love.

Then, one day, after a production meeting, I saw Boris getting ready to eat a sandwich he made for lunch. Production couldn't afford to pay for lunch every day, so the crew had to fend for themselves. This is not usually something I would write about, but like all things Boris, it was a unique experience.

Boris would take out a burgundy cloth napkin and place it on the table with fine silverware he borrowed from one of the restaurants at the racetrack. Then he would put his homemade BLT on said napkin and begin to eat his sandwich with a fork and knife. When I saw this, I thought it was a European thing, but I came to discover that it was just another strand in the tapestry that was Boris.

JIMMY'S DAILY DEBRIEFS

Every day I had to go to Jimmy's office to give him an update on how pre-production was going on. Jimmy refused to come up to the production office, which was perfectly fine with me. This was easily the worst part of my day. I would be praying in the elevator as I went down to his office. Was today going to be a good day, or was Jimmy going to threaten my life again? I'd walk in and feel the vibe in the room, telling me if it was going to be a good day or not.

Boris and I made the trek down to discuss some issues with the lighting budget. As we walked in, Jimmy was having a heated conversation with his wife, Carla. All of a sudden, Jimmy exploded on Carla. I mean he went absolutely batshit crazy. Spit was flying out of his mouth. The entire office was stunned. His face was as red as a fireball. It was like watching a car accident on the side of the road; you couldn't turn away.

I thought to myself, *If this is the way he treats his wife, what chance do I, or anyone for that matter, have?* I felt like the walls were closing in on me more and more every day.

For the first time, Boris saw the true Jimmy. After Carla started crying and ran out of the office, Jimmy turned to us.

"Sorry you had to see that, Boris. Women just have to be put in their place sometimes. You understand, right?"

Boris didn't know what to say or do at that moment, but nodded his head.

Jimmy glared at us. "You guys need something?"

"Nope, just coming by to see how things are."

I grabbed Boris and left. While in the elevator I was shaking so hard that I couldn't hide the stress anymore. Boris put his hand on my shoulder and said, "Don't worry, my friend. We are here to make a movie. I've known men like Jimmy all my life. He's a barker, not a biter."

"How do you know?"

"In my country, I knew real gangsters. People who would kill you for just looking at them in the wrong way, then put your body in a steel drum with acid to get rid of the evidence. Jimmy is not that guy. I knew guys that would eat Jimmy alive. I'm not impressed."

"You have no idea what I've been through with this guy," I told him. "I'm stressed out beyond belief. I don't know if I can do this, Boris."

At that moment Boris took me under his wing and began to carry me through pre-production. He was my saving grace. He kept me going. Weeks had gone by, and there are only so many times you can discuss the same scene. By this point of the production, I was emotionally and physically defeated. The daily verbal abuse from Jimmy was taking its toll. Boris understood what I was going through, and he became my support system, along with Frank.

THE CRITERION SESSIONS

We soon became bored out of our minds. Boris insisted I needed to watch a list of foreign films before we could work together. Every day we would lock ourselves in my office, open the laptop, and watch DVDs of old foreign films. He called our daily screenings the Criterion Sessions, named after the amazing LaserDisc and DVD film distributor of classic foreign and domestic cinema: The Criterion Collection.

He would sit there and act as my own personal commentary track, teaching me about world cinema, camera angles, lighting, and lenses. I watched thousands of films by that point in my life, but I rarely ever watched foreign films. He would say, "You have to understand what has been done before so you can learn, appreciate, and create your own. Learn from the masters, my friend."

And that's what I did. Boris introduced me to the French New Wave, Kurosawa, Kieslowski, Truffaut, Tarkovsky, Italian neorealism, Bergman, Fellini, Leone, and many more. For weeks Boris and I would watch films and break them down, analyze them, and become inspired. I was being exposed to an entirely new cinematic world.

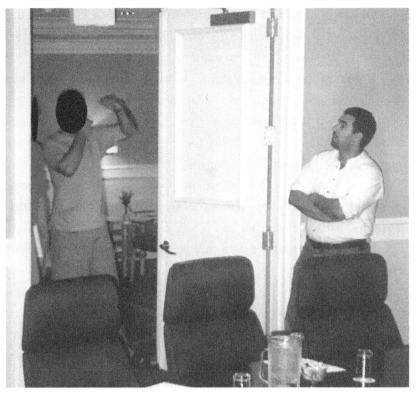

Boris showing me his ideas for covering a scene during the Criterion Sessions

Honestly, this was often the best part of my day. Boris became my mentor in many ways. He introduced me to new concepts, films, and life experiences I never would've been exposed to. My cinematic palette was broadening. I was becoming a better filmmaker.

Along with the Criterion Sessions, I returned the favor to Boris and introduced him to films he never heard of. After all, I did spend four years in a video store. Boris would come over to my place throughout the weekend, and we would just watch movies all day.

While Boris introduced me to the highbrow world of international cinema, I introduced him to the world of '80s and '90s American action films and independent cinema. We would analyze camera movements, lenses, lighting, and performance. This was the best film school in the world.

One day, after an especially brutal meeting with Jimmy, I came into the office about to burst into tears. The stress was finally breaking me. Boris came in and shut the door.

"I can't do this anymore, Boris," I said. "How can I direct a film when I'm being ripped apart every day by a psychopath?"

"My friend, I understand. All you can do is focus on the work. Why don't we create our shot list for the movie? This will keep you focused on the film and keep your mind off Jimmy."

For the next week that's all we did. Every morning I would come in, watch Boris make cappuccinos for everyone, and then we would sit down and bang out the shot list. It was like meditation for me. Boris was there every step of the way, pulling me along. Within a week we had a kick-ass shot list for the film.

Even when you might be in your darkest hours in life, the universe sends you help; an angel. For me that angel came in the form of a large eastern-European man who sounded a bit like Borat and had a cappuccino fetish. I wouldn't have had it any other way.

JIMMY GETS AN ASSISTANT

A few months into the project, Jimmy decided that he needed an assistant. All big-time producers had one; why shouldn't he? It was more for show than about actually needing help. To be honest, Jimmy would sit in his office on the second floor talking and laughing with Sid, Sam, and whichever retired gangster decided to hang out that day. I realized the retired wise guys didn't really have much to do during a typical day. I guess this movie was Jimmy's retirement plan.

Jimmy interviewed a bunch of women for the job. God-forbid he hire a male assistant. Out of all the women he interviewed Jennie stood out. She was a ball-busting New Yorker who happened to be gay. As you can imagine, Jimmy wasn't the most open-minded person when it came to race or LGBTQ rights. Back in the early 2000s we were still far away from LGBTQ acceptance, and considering Jimmy still lived in the '50s, he was nowhere close.

For some reason, Jimmy hired her. He liked having a strong woman around who wouldn't take any shit from the peanut gallery in his office. She would give just as much as she would take. Jennie was in her mid-thirties and came to the film business late in life. She didn't know what she wanted to do in the industry yet, so she wanted to try a little bit of everything.

Jennie and Jimmy had good and bad days. They would go back and forth on everything. Jimmy must've loved the challenge because she stuck around for a while.

THE BUDGET

If you remember, we started off with a $20 million budget for this opus. Then $8 million, and now it was down to $5 million. As the weeks and months went by the budget shrank, again and again. Sid reworked the budget on a weekly basis.

Every time an agent would hang up on Jimmy, or another deal for money fell through, he would have Sid drop the budget. This would cause havoc upstairs for my team and me. When the budget changed, we had to adjust everything. Each department would have to slash things from their budget. I would have to reschedule the entire film with Frank. It was a nightmare, not to mention what it did for team morale.

Jimmy pulled me into his office one day and told me, "Listen, kid, we are going to have to drop your salary on the film again. We are going to put down $25K instead of $50K in the budget. You'll be deferring the rest. Capeesh?"

"Listen, you cocksucker. I'm already owed thousands of dollars in back pay from working on this godforsaken movie. You've been busting my ass for months now. Literally torturing me on a daily basis. Belittling me in front of strangers, my crew, and my team. And now you want to cut my already-insulting salary in half because you have no fucking idea what you are doing and are destroying people's lives in order to feed your insanely over-inflated fucking ego. Is that what you are telling me? You know what, go fuck yourself, Jimmy!"

If I had said those words, that would have been amazing, but what I really said was, "Sure, Jimmy, anything to make the film happen."

You have to understand, on a $5 million film the director would normally get five to eight percent of the total budget, but since I was a first-time director $250K to $350K would be average and fair.

Jimmy offered me $50K to start, which was an insult, but hell, it was my big break, right? Now, he wanted to take the little bit of salary I had and cut it in half. I'm not even going into what was owed to me on pre-production.

***

Why did I put up with this treatment? Why didn't I just leave? A few reasons:

1. I was young, inexperienced, and had no one to guide me through this.

2. I didn't have enough self-worth at the time to demand better treatment. Jimmy never treated Boris or Frank like he treated me. They demanded a level of respect. I had no idea how to do that.

3. I was chasing my dream, this magical thing I'd read about in books and had seen in behind-the-scenes videos on DVDs and LaserDiscs. From mythical stories of Robert Rodriguez being twenty-three years old and getting a big Hollywood deal to Steven Spielberg lying to get on the Universal Studios lot and landing a studio contract.

Hollywood is a master of selling the sizzle, but most of the time the steak isn't that good or even there at all. They promote fabulous stories of actors being discovered at a diner, writers who have never written before winning Oscars, and directors getting deals off a student film. Yes, it happens, but those are the exceptions, not the norm.

The state lottery always shows you the winner, but they never show you the millions who didn't win. They sell you hope. Hope that you can make it, that you can get there, too. Hope is amazing—hell, it's needed to make it through the day sometimes—but I realize now that you need a dash of realism to accompany that hope. Balance is the key. Go for the dream, but keep your eyes open.

After years of watching the lottery winners, the story I told myself was that this was it—this was my shot. If I could just stomach Jimmy and hang tight, all my dreams would come true. I wanted to be that lottery winner, and if I had to eat a bit of shit along the way, so be it.

I went off on a tangent there, but I believe you needed to hear that to understand where I was coming from and why I didn't leave this toxic environment.

OK, back to the story.

THE INSULT

As Jimmy kept getting rejected by agent after agent, he looked for someone or something to blame. In his mind it couldn't be himself, his behavior, or his story. It couldn't be the way he screamed at the top of his lungs at agents who didn't grant him access to their clients. So it must be the script.

I'd worked for months getting the screenplay to a place where we could shoot. I polished the hell out of that script. Everyone who read it loved the new version. At first Jimmy told me he loved it as well, but because he had no idea how to evaluate a professional screenplay, his views could change on a dime. Jimmy called me into his office and told me he made an appointment to meet with a script consultant.

"I think the script is the reason I'm not getting the traction I want."

"OK, if you feel that way, I'm open to hearing what he has to say."

"You are cute, kid. You make it sound like there's a choice in the matter."

"Who is it?"

"He teaches screenwriting at the local college."

I understand bringing in a Hollywood script doctor to tighten up and re-work the script—hell, most screenplays in the business receive this treatment—but to bring in a guy who teaches screenwriting at a local community college was an insult.

After doing research on him I found out that he had never sold a screenplay, never stepped foot in Los Angeles, had no industry contacts, and basically taught how to format screenplays. Might as well have taken the screenplay to a dentist for notes. I went along with it since I really didn't have a choice.

We met the guy at his office on campus. As Jimmy and I walked into his office the smell of old gym socks filled the air. Screenplays were stacked to the ceiling. Jimmy poked me and pointed to the screenplays, "You see, this guy is the real deal."

Speechless, just speechless.

We sat down to discuss the film with him. He had read the script and had a bunch of notes, none of which made much sense. I have no issue collaborating or taking notes on anything I work on, but they have to be of value to the story. These had no such value. Most of the notes were there just to show Jimmy he did something. I found out later that this guy had to justify the $3,000 price tag he was charging for the rewrite. Remember, I hadn't been paid a dime for all the work I put into the screenplay.

I sat there listening to this guy spew out nonsense. Breaking down the hero's journey in a way that made no sense, but the dog-and-pony show worked on Jimmy. We now had a new, updated script that we had to re-budget and reschedule. The team was going to love this. We walked back to Jimmy's car.

"That guy knew what he was talking about, right?"

"I didn't like any of his ideas."

"Come on, kid, don't let your ego get in the way of making a great movie."

Did he just say that to me? Jimmy had absolutely no self-awareness at all. What was I going to say? Sure, why not? Let's change everything, again. At least it would keep us busy for a while longer.

SCORSESE CALLING

Jimmy always promised me that legendary film director Martin Scorsese would be involved with his project somehow. Marty is a GOD in the wise-guy world because of films like *Goodfellas, Mean Streets, Casino,* and *The Departed.* Those films helped create the mythical image of the "wise guy" in the popular culture we know today. This image of the wise guy was what Jimmy used daily to manipulate and scare people into doing what he wanted.

On my way to a production meeting Jimmy called me into his office and handed me the phone. On the other end of the line was an Oscar-nominated actor who was a staple in many of Scorsese's mob-themed films. I was shocked. Jimmy loved doing that to people, shocking and scaring the hell out of them. I think he got a high from it.

The actor and I chatted for a while.

"I read your script, and I would love to be a part of this film in any way I can. Do you have a part for me?"

I was gobsmacked.

"Of course! It would be an honor to have you in the film. I'm a huge fan of your work."

"Thank you," said the actor. "I'm humbled. Listen, I also saw the trailer you shot. Very impressive. So impressive in fact that I'm going to walk the tape into Marty's office myself and make him watch it. Would that be OK?"

I thought of words in my head, but nothing came out of mouth. I couldn't speak; it was as if my brain had seized up.

"I take it by your silence that you are fine with it?"

"Yes, yes, of course. That would be amazing."

"Excellent! Put Jimmy back on the phone. It was a pleasure speaking to you, and I look forward to working with you on this."

I thanked him again and passed the phone back to Jimmy. You could see Jimmy's eyes light up when he heard the news. He thanked the actor and hung up. Jimmy could barely contain himself. "See, I told you. Martin fuckin' Scorsese is going to watch your trailer."

Is this really happening? Is Martin Scorsese really going to watch my work? I was walking on air for the rest of the day.

These are the kinds of things that kept me in Jimmy's web. Every time I'd speak to a famous actor or meet an Oscar-winning producer, I'd say to myself, *This is happening. See, just hang in there a little bit longer.* I would talk myself into it. When you want to believe in something all you need is a little proof and you are hooked. This is the base principle of all cons.

At the end, I never heard back from anyone at Marty's office. Jimmy said he liked the trailer but was too busy to add any more films to his plate. Whether or not this was true I'll never know. As always, the sizzle was better than the actual steak.

CHAPTER 11

Endless Location Scout

We were based in a smaller city just outside of New Orleans. Every time Chip and I wanted to see a location in New Orleans Jimmy would blow a gasket.

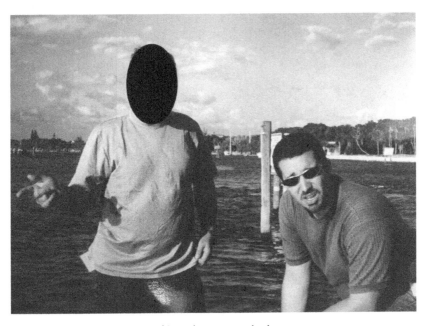

Boris and I on a location scout by the water

"I'm not giving that fucking city one dime of my money. The film commissioner over there is an asshole. I asked for help, and he said he needed 'proof of funds' before he would lift a finger. He's lucky I didn't go down to his office and straighten him out."

Of course, Jimmy had a fight with the film commissioner of the state's biggest city, home to many beautiful locations that would be perfect for the film. This made Chip's job that much harder.

There was only so much pre-production that could be done in the office, so Chip had the team and me on the road a lot. We must've seen hundreds of houses, office buildings, historic sites, and hospitals. You name it, we probably location-scouted it. The team that usually went out was me, Chip, Frank, Boris, and sometimes Jerry. This kept us busy and from going insane. Boris would always joke, "This film is like a *Hotel California*: you can check in, but you can never leave."

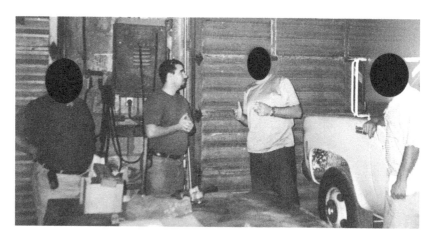

Jerry, Boris and I on a location scout

We would all load up in one of the Lexus SUVs that Dave, our product placement guy, got us. We'd pack a cooler full of food and drinks, usually paid for by me, and hit the road.

One of the highlights of the trip was using our new GPS system, which was super-advanced technology for the time. Boris was fascinated with the GPS's female voice. He called it the lady in the trunk.

"My friends, I might leave my wife for this car."

Funny thing is that these trips were life-changing for us as a team. It felt like we were escaping from the prison of this project for a while. Warden Jimmy had no control over us when we were on the road.

For Boris and Frank this was literally true. They had been living out of a hotel for months at this point. I could only imagine how they felt. Chip, Jerry, and I at least got to go home at the end of the day. They only had a hotel room with HBO to keep them warm at night. In many ways this was their prison, too.

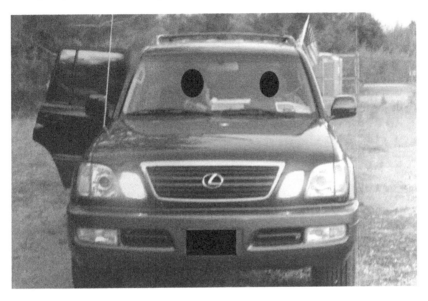

Boris, Frank in the car that Jimmy scammed for the production, with a space age GPS system

"I have to tell you, Alex," said Boris, "the hell with making Jimmy's movie! What we need to do is set up cameras around the production office and film everything. It will be the best reality show ever made. The insanity of trying to make this film with Jimmy as the producer is untapped gold, my friend."

We all laughed, but he was right. This would've made an amazing reality show. It was still a few years before Matt Damon and Ben Affleck's groundbreaking reality show about the filmmaking process,

Project Greenlight, would premier on HBO. I guess we were ahead of our time.

BLACK LIGHTS, GLITTER, AND ALL-YOU-CAN-EAT BUFFETS

One of the main locations in the film was a period strip club, so of course, the boys wanted to check out as many locations as possible. Chip would schedule us to go to these strip clubs in the middle of nowhere.

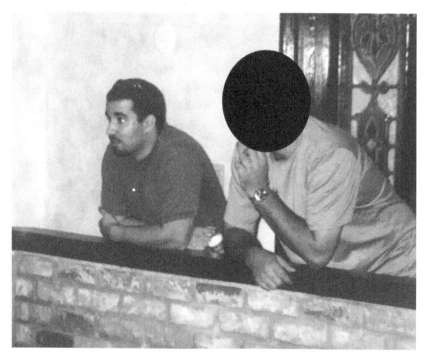

Boris and I contemplating shots in the upstairs balcony of a strip club while location scouting

The location needed to be dated, cavernous, and have an eighties vibe to it. Oddly enough, that wasn't a problem. Most of the clubs we scouted had all of this and more. Apparently, men didn't go to these places for the ambience. Some of these clubs were decades old.

There was this one strip club that I'll never forget. Chip pulled into the parking lot of this giant freestanding building near the airport, which was creatively called "Strippers." It was ridiculously big. Giant Roman pillars out front with lions at the door. It was noon, so the lunch rush was in. I use the word *rush* extremely loosely.

As I walked in, I saw what the lunch rush looked like. There must have been four guys in the entire place. The dancers outnumbered the clientele.

What stood out even more was the full buffet by the side stage. The saddest steaks you have ever seen. It was just awful. I'd truly never seen something so sad in all my life. Guys watching strippers while eating a tough-as-nails ribeye at noon on a Thursday. I felt sorry for both the clients and the employees.

Looking past the obviously sad situation, we began to actually location scout the place. It looked like a time capsule from the eighties. Gold trim dripped off the walls. Mirrors with glitter wrapped around the entirety of the room. There was a second floor where the dancers descended from to the main stage. In all honesty, the place was perfect. It would cost us tens of thousands of dollars to try to recreate this place on a soundstage.

Boris asked, "Is this what Americans call strip club?"

Until that day, Boris had never been inside a strip club before. He was as blown away as I was. He looked past the sadness and started to see where he could place lights, check the main breaker for power, etc.

I told Chip that Boris and I loved the location. Of course, that didn't stop Chip from showing us more clubs in the weeks to come, even if we didn't want to see any more. I think Chip was enjoying his job a bit too much.

THE 1%

What would a film about gangsters be without ridiculously over-the-top mansions? Chip put us on the road scouting some of the largest houses I had ever seen.

We walked into one house where the owner was an art collector. He literally had millions of dollars of ugly art covering every inch of the walls. It looked so tacky.

They had an elevator in the house and a dining room table made entirely of a rare Italian blue marble. The table was so large and heavy he said if they sold the house it would have to stay or the insurance wouldn't cover it. The entire experience didn't compute in my mind. I was a middle-class kid who only saw stuff like this in television and movies.

The one mansion that stood out was my trip to the lottery winners'. This couple won the state lottery a few years back. They won $75 million to be exact. This mansion must've been ten thousand square feet, and it sat on a twenty-acre property. On the outside was all metal siding, and the inside was covered in old, dark mahogany. It just made no sense. Two completely different styles.

The main thing Boris, Chip, and I noticed when we walked into the place was the smell. There were at least a hundred cats roaming the house. Kitty litter boxes everywhere. It turned out this couple lived in a trailer park before their financial windfall. A framed picture of their double-wide trailer adorned their wall.

They had a collection of international Coke cans, refrigerator magnets, and spoons. They apparently loved to travel. The backyard was a mini water park, including statues of lions and tigers in the water. The owners were extremely arrogant and were really just there to show off. I thought they would be a nightmare to work with if we picked their house.

We continued to scout mansion after mansion. Huge and beautiful homes, but in many ways sadder than the strip clubs with the disgusting buffets. All that money, all that space, for two or three people—just seemed like a waste.

IS THAT A CANDLE IN A COSTCO CHICKEN?

After coming back from a long day of location scouting, Frank was complaining about his back and that he was too old for this kind of stuff anymore. Little did he know that Boris and I set up a surprise for him.

We turned the corner into our office, and the entire gang was sitting around his desk. Everyone yelled out, "Happy birthday, Frank!"

Frank was completely taken off guard. Jimmy started singing the "Happy Birthday" song, and everyone joined in. As Frank got closer to his desk, he noticed that the birthday cake wasn't actually a cake—it was a Costco chicken with a candle in it. Frank couldn't stop talking about Costco chickens when he was on the road with us, so Boris and I thought this would be a perfect gift for him.

Frank couldn't have been happier. He blew out the candle and said, "Thank you, all, for this. I really needed it. I miss home something terribly, but this has brightened up my day."

Jimmy smirked, "You deserve it. A fuckin' candle in a chicken, who knew?"

Everyone cracked up.

Frank noticed Jimmy's ridiculously expensive wristwatch. "Jimmy, that's a beautiful watch. I used to have a similar one years ago, just without the upgrades." And he laughed.

Jimmy saw there was a stage where he could perform. The entire crew was around having drinks and celebrating.

"Frank, if you like it, it's yours." He made sure he spoke loud enough for everyone to hear.

Jimmy took off the watch and handed it to Frank.

"Jimmy, are you crazy? I can't accept a gift like this."

"Take my gift, Frank. You deserve it."

"I just can't take it."

"Don't insult me. It's yours."

Frank looked in Jimmy's eyes and knew he meant it. Everyone was watching the exchange go down. If Frank refused the gift, Jimmy would look bad, and you don't want Jimmy to look bad.

"Thank you, Jimmy, for this generous gift."

"You deserve this and more, Frank. Thank you for helping make my dream come true with this movie."

He took the watch, and everyone in the room clapped. Jimmy, smoking a cigar, hugged Frank and then had a drink.

We all ate from the weirdest birthday cake we'd ever seen, but Frank was happy and that's all that mattered. He was the glue that held the production together, the patriarch of the film. Whenever Jimmy was on a rampage Frank was the only one who could calm him down. For some reason Frank had that power. Jimmy respected Frank in a way he didn't respect anyone else.

I had Frank speak to Jimmy on my behalf more times than I care to remember. Jimmy never yelled or threatened me, or anyone for that matter, in front of Frank. I guess Frank represented something to Jimmy that touched him to his core. After all, Frank had been on and off the Jimmy crazy train for years.

GOING TO THE BIG HOUSE

Every gangster movie has a scene in a prison, and our story was no exception. I must have been inside every minimum-security prison across three states. I was extremely uneasy walking into a prison, even though I knew I was going to walk out. Once those doors closed behind me, a chill would run up my spine.

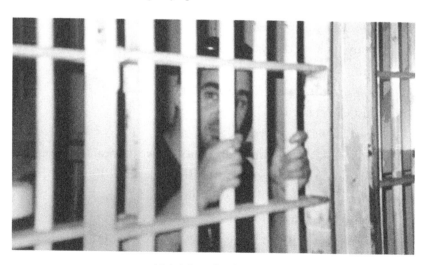

Me in jail on a location scout

Some of the prisons were old and worn down by time, while others were brand new. Seeing how they housed prisoners in these facilities was sad and jarring. I've seen hundreds of prisons and jail scenes in films over the years. *Shawshank Redemption* is on my top five films of all time, of course.

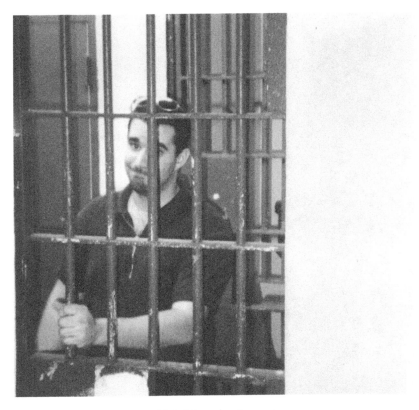

Me in jail on a location scout

It's one thing to watch it, and another to walk through and see it firsthand, smelling the stale air and seeing where prisoners ate and slept. The hopelessness of the situation permeates your soul. I wanted to make sure I did my best to translate that feeling onto the screen. Boris, Frank, and Chip were all uneasy in these places. Frank wanted to get in and get out as soon as possible, and I didn't blame him.

In one of the prisons we visited, I was invited to go into one of the cells. As I walked in, I could feel the tightness of the walls. The sound the door made when it shut behind me will stick with me 'til the day I die. I felt the hopelessness of the situation, being in a place where I had no power, no way to escape.

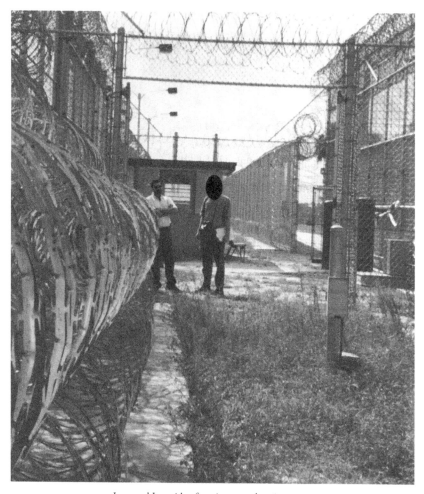

Jerry and I outside of a prison on a location scout

As the boys and I would walk around the facility I couldn't help but see the parallels between walking those prison halls and walking the racetrack halls. One had walls, guards, and barbwire; the other had Jimmy. Both were prisons, just of different makings.

I'VE GOT ANOTHER JOB, JIMMY

Jerry was an absolute professional. He really wasn't very personable or there to make friends. He did his job and that was it. I invited him and Boris out one night for drinks, and there we discovered the reason why he was like he was.

For Boris, filmmaking was his life, his dream, and his first love. For Jerry, being a production designer was just a job. Like going to a nine-to-five and punching a clock. He enjoyed what he was doing, but it was by no means a passion.

It had been weeks since anyone was last paid. Jimmy's threats and false promises kept the crew at bay so far, but a big studio film had just come into town and the crew wanted in.

Jerry decided he was going to try to jump on that film for a few weeks and then come back to our movie. He asked me what I thought, and I gave him my full support. Next step was to go downstairs and ask Jimmy if it was OK.

"How do you think he'll respond?"

"It's fifty fifty, Jerry. I wish you the best of luck."

He went downstairs to Jimmy's office and knocked on the door.

"Jimmy, you have a minute?"

"Sure, Jerry, what can I do for you?"

"Listen, you know I love working for you and being a part of this film, but I wanted to know if I could jump onto another gig for a few weeks just to make some extra money. Since I haven't been paid for a few weeks now, I need some cash. There's a studio film that just came into town, and I was asked if I was available. What do you think?"

Jimmy's face began to turn beet red. Like a pressure cooker that was about to explode, you could see what was coming.

"Mother fucker, are you talking to me about money? How about the millions of dollars I already put into this film? Who's going to pay me back? Wait, are you going to roll on me? Are you leaving this family I put together? The family I invited you into?"

Jerry turned pale and kept saying, "No, no, no, Jimmy. I'll be back. I promise. I just need to make some money to pay rent. You understand, right?"

Jimmy got up from his chair and started yelling at the top of his lungs so everyone within earshot could hear.

"The only thing I understand, mother fucker, is that you are turning colors on me, but you know what? Sure, you can leave. Just be careful turning your car on from now on. If you hear a click, that might be your last."

"Why would you say that?"

Everyone else in the office was frozen, afraid to even move.

"Leave, leave. But I would always check under your bedsheets for snakes and your bathtub for alligators. Shit happens, but by all means, take that other job."

Poor Jerry had no idea how to react to this. He had walked into a buzz saw.

"What's wrong? Can't talk now? Cat's got your tongue?"

He mumbled out a few defeated words. "I want to see this film get made, Jimmy. I'll stay on."

"That's what I thought, mother fucker. Now walk your ass upstairs and get to work."

When I left to direct that commercial there was no crew around other than the office and me, but now it was different. Jimmy understood that if even one crew member left, then everyone would abandon ship and his con would be over. Jerry didn't take that job and lost thousands of dollars in the process. The word got around to everyone what had happened, and that's what Jimmy wanted—to make an example out of Jerry.

The crew would stay together for a little longer, but if Jimmy couldn't find cash to keep the boat afloat, then no amount of screaming and threats would keep the crew on.

IS THAT MONEY BURNT?

Money was getting pretty light around the racetrack offices. The crew hadn't been paid in weeks, and Jimmy was reaching the end of his rope unless he could find some cash, and quick.

Francisco, being the opportunist that he was, offered Jimmy a deal. Francisco had worked on an independent film financed completely by Jamaican businessmen. Let's use the term *businessmen* extremely loosely. He set up a meeting with Jimmy and the Jamaicans, but demanded an associate producer credit on the film if everything went well. Jimmy reluctantly agreed.

(By the way, an associate producer credit means absolutely nothing in the film industry. It is given as a token to people who did a little extra on a film or as a bargaining chip for actors, writers, money guys, etc.)

Later that week Francisco brought two large Jamaican Rastafarians to meet with Jimmy in his office. They looked like they just walked off stage at a Bob Marley concert. Dreadlocks swinging in the air. The smell of ganja filled the room.

Jimmy looked at them with a bit of disdain in his eyes. Let's just say that Jimmy's views on race were a bit outdated. He didn't particularly like dealing with people who had darker skin, but considering he was desperate, he did what he needed to.

The Jamaicans sat down with a large black bag in tow. Jimmy went into his regular sales pitch, and the Jamaicans looked impressed. He walked them upstairs to our office, where he introduced me and the rest of the gang. Francisco stood behind everyone, looking like a Chihuahua waiting for a treat.

Jimmy showed them the look wall, which was easily the most impressive thing in the room. I spoke to them about my plans for the film, referring to movies I loved in the genre, and how unique this story was. Boris came out and discussed lighting, cameras, and the look of the movie. The Jamaicans ate up the dog-and-pony show. Jimmy praised himself as the producer that put this entire thing together.

They all went back down to Jimmy's office to discuss details. After about fifteen minutes, the Jamaicans shook everyone's hands and walked out, leaving the bag behind. I came in and saw Jimmy with a smile from ear to ear.

"How'd it go, Jimmy?"

"Don't worry. I closed them, kid." Jimmy slapped a bag of money on the desk. "They left us a small deposit, but they'll be financing the rest of the budget next week."

I looked in the bag and saw nothing but hundred-dollar bills.

Francisco was standing there looking for some bit of gratitude from Jimmy.

"You've done good, Francisco. Now, everybody get back to work."

Later that day everyone on the crew got an envelope full of cash. It was back pay for a few weeks. Well below what we were owed, but it was something. Boris opened his envelope, and as he counted his money, he noticed something. He came over to me. "My friend, do you see this?"

I looked down and saw that a few of the hundred-dollar bills were burnt and had some red speckles on them. Jesus Christ!

"Boris, just take it to the bank and don't look back."

A few days later, we all discovered that the rest of the financing had fallen through again. It turned out that our Jamaican saviors had been arrested for some illegal use of force in another deal. Jimmy's anger could not be contained. He called and called, but Francisco didn't pick up. Francisco was nowhere to be found. You could hear Jimmy yelling profanities downstairs that I won't repeat here.

Once Francisco heard what happened, he knew his time was up on the production, or maybe even up for good. He took off and left town, not to be heard from again.

That was the one positive thing about the entire situation—no more Francisco. He'd brought me into this nightmare, and now he had his own nightmare to deal with, looking over his shoulder for years to come. Karma is a bitch.

WHY DON'T YOU JUST LEAVE?

I know many of you reading this right now are saying, "I would've just left. The hell with Jimmy and his BS. I wouldn't put up with that."

That's easy for you to say. It's completely different when you are in the shit, seeing and feeling a gangster threaten you and your friends. Maybe I just didn't have the strength or courage to stand up for myself, and that's probably true. Even after all the threats, stress, and abuse I was still there, but why? I asked myself that question for years to come. Hell, I'm still asking that question today as I write this book.

The allure of making my dreams come true was extremely powerful. So powerful that I put up with a level of crap that most people wouldn't. I mean, I was meeting Hollywood players. It felt so close, like at any second it would all come together and I would be off living that dream that Hollywood sells so well.

I guess it's like being in an abusive relationship. You believe the person you are with is the one you have been dreaming about all your life. Sure, he or she isn't perfect, but you'll put up with the negatives because the positives are so amazing. Sooner or later the positives become overshadowed by the negatives. What was once a dream come true becomes a nightmare. That's where I was in this part of my story.

Just when you think to yourself, *I'm going to leave this situation because it isn't good for me anymore*, your partner does something so great that you forget the negatives for a while longer and you stay in a horrible relationship.

That super-positive thing was about to happen with me in this toxic relationship. My second trip to Hollyweird was just around the corner. My dream of directing a Hollywood feature film was finally coming true. That's what I kept telling myself at least.

CHAPTER 12

Back to Hollyweird

After months of location scouting, prepping the movie, and what seemed to be an endless production meeting, some good news was about to come in. Jimmy called me into his office one day. In Jimmy fashion, he made the news extremely dramatic.

"So, kid, I have a question for you. Do you watch TV?"

"Of course I do, Jimmy."

"Do you watch *Friends?*"

"Yes, that's, like, one of my favorite shows."

"Would you like to go on the set of that show?"

"Jesus, Jimmy, you're killing me. What's going on?"

"OK, OK. We are flying to Los Angeles tomorrow to meet one of the main actors on the set of *Friends*."

Could this really be happening?

"Go pack your bags and bring something respectable so I won't be embarrassed when I introduce you."

I thought to myself, *Embarrassed? Have you looked in the mirror lately, Jimmy?* Before I packed, I told the gang what was happening. There was an electricity in the room, a feeling of hope, as if this film might finally get made.

BACK TO HOLLYWEIRD

I found myself walking with Jimmy in the airport again, rushing to make the flight. We were getting our usual looks, as Jimmy is dressed in his favorite flying outfit: solid-gold tracksuit, gold chains draped over his wife beater, and, of course, a black hat with a feather popping out. Even the gate attendant looked at Jimmy and gave a giggle as we walked onto the plane.

When we strapped into our seats, I noticed that Jimmy was a bit more nervous than usual. Remember, Jimmy hated flying because he thought "wicked people" shouldn't fly. I took advantage of that knowledge and jumped from my seat.

"Jimmy! What was that sound?"

"Kid, I swear, shut the fuck up!"

"Seriously, Jimmy, I think I heard a part from the wing just fall off."

"I'm not listening to you, mother fucker. Once this Ambien kicks in I'll be good."

He put on his noise-cancelling headphones and closed his eyes. I laughed to myself. My relationship with Jimmy was so strange. On one side I was deathly afraid of his bipolar and unpredictable homicidal tendencies, and on the other I felt it was OK to tease him about one of his greatest fears.

Jimmy was one way in public and another in private. I had long conversations with him where there were no threats or bullying. We were just two guys talking. He had to put on his persona in public to survive the world he came from. If you show weakness, you're dead. He just had a problem turning that part of himself off.

When we got to Hollywood, we went to the world-famous Jerry's Deli and had a quick bite. We started talking about how Jimmy got caught and put in jail. I knew the story a bit but wanted to know the whole truth.

"Jimmy, how did you really get snagged by the cops?"

"What I'm going to tell you does not make it into the movie, capeesh?"

"Of course, Jimmy."

"I was fingered by this teenager who ratted me out. He witnessed a job I did years ago."

"So how did that kid make it to testify? Didn't your crew take him out?"

"You watch too many movies, kid. It was the day of the trial, and I was in the bathroom before I was going to go in and face the judge. I look over and the kid who ratted on me comes out of the stall. I looked at him, and, I shit you not, he pissed his pants, which must've been tough since he just went to the john. I told him that we were good. That nothing was going to happen to him."

"Why would you let that fly?"

"You think I was going to kill a young kid for ratting me out? What kind of animal do you think I am? I still live by the old rules—no women, no children. Something these fucking Russians don't understand."

At that moment I understood Jimmy a bit more. He lived by a code. No matter how screwed up that code might be, it was his code.

"I had a friendly sit-down with a group of Russian bastards once. They were being a bit cocky about how they were taking control of territories from the Italians. I turned to that mother fucker and said, 'When you run things for one hundred years, then come talk to me.' Everyone at that table busted out laughing. Fucking Russians, they have no code, no honor."

It was amazing to hear Jimmy talk about code and honor. I guess this was the story he told himself to get to sleep at night. I always wondered how bad people could live with themselves after doing horrific things daily. It's the stories they tell themselves to cope. No one sees himself as the villain of his own story, and Jimmy was a perfect example of that.

The next morning, we jumped into a cab to head over to the set of *Friends* to meet the actor. This was my second time in Los Angeles, and I was still in awe. We were driving through Beverly Hills, and everywhere I looked all I saw was the film biz. Production companies on every corner, big post-production houses, and sound stages covered the landscape. I recognized locations from television shows and movies. Was that the hotel from *Pretty Woman*? Well, yes it was. I was truly in heaven.

I turned to my left and saw Bugs Bunny on the top of a building; then I saw the Warner Brothers water tower. We had arrived. As we drove to the main entrance, we passed two-story posters of the studio's latest films and television shows. As we pulled into the entrance where they shot the big scene from *Blazing Saddles*, my heart began to beat a bit faster than usual.

"Ready for the big time, kid? Now, don't embarrass me."

We pulled up to the guard house, and Jimmy gave our names to security.

"Sorry, sir, but you are not on the list," the guard apologized.

"That's impossible, check again."

The guard checked again, but no go. Jimmy started to lose his temper.

"Check the fucking list again."

This time the guard said, "Sir, please turn around and leave the lot."

Jimmy began to curse out this poor guard, yelling at the top of his lungs, "I have a drive-on for *Friends*! Don't you know who the fuck I am?"

"If you were anyone you wouldn't be driving on the lot in a taxi, sir," the guard replied.

Jimmy lost his mind. Three other security guards came up and instructed the taxi driver to turn the car around and leave. The driver obeyed.

I had seen Jimmy upset hundreds of times before, but this was a new level. His eyeballs looked as if they were going to explode out of his skull. He was almost foaming at the mouth.

Jimmy had the taxi driver drop us off at a nearby In-N-Out burger joint. Pacing outside, he called the actor's agent, the guy who set this entire meeting up.

"Wait a minute, what do you mean he's not available? I flew all night to meet this mutha fucker."

He was not handling the news well.

"I don't give a fuck that his grandmother died. Get me the meeting you fucking promised me, or send me a check for the money I dished out for this trip. I'm not going to eat this, you little shit. I should head over to your office right now and straighten you out for good, you little fucking cock-sucker."

The agent had enough and hung up on him. Jimmy couldn't contain himself. I just kept quiet and out of his line of sight. He made a few more calls while pacing and cursing up a storm behind the restaurant.

Just another day on the world's most insane film production. One minute you are about to meet one of the biggest television stars in the world on the Warner Brothers lot, and the next you are yelling into a phone in the back of an In-N-Out in Studio City. This is the real Hollywood.

After the incident with the actor's agent, Jimmy had a tougher time getting any big agencies or agents on the phone. Believe it or not, Hollywood is a small town, and word gets around. You can't yell and threaten an agent without having yourself and your project blacklisted. Jimmy didn't get that agents at that level can't be spoken to that way, but he learned quickly.

Now the only way to get any kind of major talent attached to the project was going to be through a reputable producer with some juice in town. We had a few of those kinds of guys left on our side, for now.

I DIDN'T KNOW DIRECTORS PISSED THEIR PANTS

After Jimmy cooled down a bit, we went back to the Sofitel Hotel in Beverly Hills, where we always stayed while visiting Los Angeles. Jimmy and I went shopping across the street at the Beverly Center, looking for the perfect gift for another meeting lined up that night.

We were meeting with a legendary actor that Jimmy wanted to have play a major part in the film. Of course, he wouldn't tell me his name, so I would be in the dark until that night. Jimmy loved that sense of showmanship, keeping people guessing. I hated it.

He settled on a box of Cuban cigars from this fancy cigar shop. The owner of the shop pulled it out of the back since they were still illegal to own in the United States. Jimmy and the owner apparently went way back.

Later that night, we arrived at this Beverly Hills restaurant with a line out the door. All I saw were Ferraris, Bentleys, Porsches, and limos pulling up. Of course, we were dropped off in a cab, but that didn't matter. Jimmy walked up to the door, pulled out a huge money clip, and tipped the guy a hundred. Magically, we had no issues and walked right in, skipping everyone.

Once inside it was like a '90s Planet Hollywood opening. There were stars everywhere. Sylvester Stallone was having dinner with Bruce Willis. *Is that Jean-Claude Van Damme?* It was completely nuts. The maître d' had us wait at the bar as he prepared a table. Apparently, we were not just meeting this legendary actor, but Boris's agent was also coming. This was going to be fun.

While we waited, I saw one of the hottest young directors in the world walk in the front door. We'll call him "Tony." I studied this guy's work while I was in college. He was on an unprecedented run of hit film after hit film. He was Hollywood's new golden boy. I really couldn't believe it. Movie stars were nice, but I was more interested in meeting filmmakers.

I nudged Jimmy and pointed him out of the small crowd gathered at the front door. Jimmy looked over, and a sinister smile appeared on his face.

"Hey, kid, want to see a big film director piss his pants?"

"What do you mean?"

"Watch this."

Jimmy walked up to him and said, "Hey, Tony!"

Tony looked over at Jimmy.

"How are you doing, kid? How's that limp doing?"

I had never seen fear race onto someone's face so fast before. Tony went white and started to physically shake.

"Oh, hi, Ji-Ji-Jimmy. How-how-how are things, things?"

"Still haven't gotten rid of the fucking stutter yet?"

Tony started to slowly back away from us.

"Gotta-gotta-go-go, Jimmy. Nice to-to see you again."

He turned around and bolted for the door, where he ran into his supermodel girlfriend. I could see Tony telling his confused girlfriend that they had to go and then pulling her out of the restaurant.

"Why do you have to leave so soon?"

Jimmy couldn't stop laughing. I was confused as hell.

"What just happened?"

"Me and Tony go way back. Years ago, when he was a cocky prick running around the clubs, I had a run-in with him."

I was all ears.

"That stuttering prick came from money, so he thought he could do anything he wanted to anyone he wanted. He came into a bar where me and a few of my boys always had drinks. Tony walks in with a few of his frat friends and started making a scene. You could tell he was running on tequila and coke. He was annoying one of the bartenders, trying to pick her up. This little fuck literally pulled out his cock and slapped it on the bar in front of her. I went over and slammed him to the floor and gave him a Billy Bates[8] beating."

I was speechless.

"My boys had to pull me off him before I went too far. That kid never forgot me—that, I can promise you, as you saw tonight. Little prick."

He started laughing again. Jimmy never failed to surprise, entertain, or scare the shit out of you.

We were shown to our table. I sat down, looked to my left, and saw that the legendary Jerry Lee Lewis[9] and Harry Dean Stanton[10] were eating dinner next to us. I swear, I was in a dream.

Soon after, Eva, Boris's agent, joined us. She was tall, beautiful, well educated, and spoke with a thick eastern European accent. As she

---

[8] *Character from Goodfellas*
[9] *Musician who wrote "Great Balls of Fire"*
[10] *Actor from Alien and The Green Mile*

spoke to Jimmy you could see her fascination with him grow. Boris was reporting back all the craziness from the racetrack, and Eva just had to see if the stories were true.

Of course, Jimmy didn't disappoint. He jumped right into stories of his old days as a gangster, and Eva was hooked. She gaped at him as if she were watching a freak show, in awe of the crazy.

Our main guest finally arrived. We'll call him "The Legend." The Legend sat down at the table, and the energy changed immediately. He had a regal presence to him and was extremely gracious. The Legend introduced himself to the entire table, even though everyone in the restaurant knew who he was. I remember watching him in some of the biggest films of the day. He's known as an actor's actor, and it would be a dream come true to direct him in any film.

Jimmy's energy also changed. He became a fanboy all of a sudden, quoting lines from his films, asking him what it was like to work with legendary actresses and actors of his day. It was a bit much, but that was Jimmy. The Legend played along, as I'm sure this happens to him on a daily basis.

The Legend finally asked me what my vision was for Jimmy's film. I went into the overall vision and what I wanted his character to be, and broke down scenes. The one thing I asked him was, "How do you like to be directed?"

When working with a legendary actor who obviously knows how to act, it's my job as the director to guide his performance, but that needs to be tailored to each actor, and The Legend was no different. He was taken aback when I asked him that.

"You know, after all these years working with the biggest directors in the business no one has ever asked me that before."

I became a bit nervous. Had I inadvertently offended him? You could see Jimmy's face change as he said that. The anger started to bubble up.

"Thank you for asking me."

The tension left my shoulders. Jimmy relaxed. The Legend then discussed his process and how we could collaborate on the film.

"Jimmy, you picked a good man here. A real diamond in the rough."

I was honored and a bit shocked by his praise.

"Can I pick them or what? I also have another surprise for you." Jimmy pulled out the box of Cuban Cigars and handed it to him. The Legend acted taken aback, but I could tell he was used to people giving him gifts.

"Cohibas are your favorite, right?"

"They are, Jimmy. Thank you for this, but you didn't have to do this."

"My pleasure," Jimmy said beaming.

We finished our meal. Eva had been a fly on the wall throughout the dinner, simply in awe of the scene she just witnessed.

"My people will be in touch."

The Legend got up and left. Jimmy was so happy he could barely contain himself. Eva also left and thanked Jimmy for the evening.

"Don't worry, we'll take good care of Boris for you."

Eva gave him an unconvincing smile and walked away. I felt she had Jimmy's number from the moment she sat down at the table.

"See, kid, do I disappoint? Stick with me and you'll be working with movie stars bigger than him."

I also gave Jimmy an unconvincing smile.

The amazing thing about Jimmy was that he was a con man for sure, but he was able to get things like this to happen. Meeting Oscar-winning actors, scaring the crap out of one of Hollywood's biggest directors—all these things that made you believe he was for real, that he could actually pull this film off.

Even though I was being verbally threatened on an almost-daily basis, that shiny carrot hung just out of my reach. I could see it there, and at times I could almost touch it, tonight being one of those times, before it would be pulled away again. That was the danger of the situation. You keep putting up with all sorts of crap with the promise that you'll get your dream. You can spend a lifetime being this dumb, and trust me, I almost did.

JERRY'S DELI

One of the staples of every trip to Los Angeles with Jimmy was a visit to the world-famous Jerry's Deli. I spent time in New York, so I know what a good Jewish deli is, and Jerry's is one of the best. Jimmy and I would have breakfast there almost every morning when we were in town.

Jimmy liked to set up morning meetings at Jerry's. One morning we had a meeting with an Oscar-winning sound designer whom we will call "The Fox." Jimmy wasn't only looking to stack the front of the camera—the credits behind the camera were just as important. Credits and awards meant everything to Jimmy. The bigger the credit, the better, and of course, if you had an Oscar nomination, that was gold in Jimmy's eyes.

Creating that smoke-and-mirror facade was part of Jimmy's con. He needed anything he could get to legitimize his film project, and I was definitely not going to help him trick these people.

We sat with The Fox and spoke about post-production, his work-flow, and how it felt to be nominated for an Oscar. Since I came from a post-production background, we could speak the same language. Jimmy was asking him all sorts of questions.

By the end of the meal The Fox was pitching himself for the job, hard. That was the first time I realized that you can't cash-in an Oscar award at the bank. The award won't pay your mortgage or buy you food. The Fox and his team had to hustle just like the rest of us. Sure, an Oscar will open the door, but the hustle has to be there. Especially for below-the-line crew.

I'LL TAKE YOU. JUST JUMP IN MY TRUCK

I got a call as we walked out of the meeting. "It's Harry!" I told Jimmy that we should have a coffee with Harry the next time we were in Los Angeles, considering what an amazing job he did starring in our little trailer.

Harry told us to meet him at this coffee shop in Westwood. We jumped in a taxi and headed over. When we got there Harry was already waiting in a long line. We hugged.

"How the hell are you doing, mate?"

"Doing well, just running around taking meetings with Jimmy."

Jimmy, as if on cue, walked in.

"How the hell are you, Harry?"

Harry said hello. His energy was infectious. He was wearing his trademark Hawaiian shirt, cargo shorts, and sandals. We ordered and headed to a table outside.

"How's it going, boys?"

"Great! We are finalizing some actors as we speak and hope to start shooting in a few weeks."

Did Jimmy know something I didn't? I think when liars lie, they get so used to lying that it becomes second nature to them. Jimmy spurted out lies like water from a hose, and it didn't even faze him.

"The kid here has a meeting with a big-time star this afternoon. Just waiting to see what time they are going to meet."

News to me. I had no idea if he was telling the truth or just bull-shitting Harry as-usual.

"That's awesome! I hope you can find a small part for a humble actor from England to play."

Jimmy laughed. "Of course, Harry. You are one of the guys who got us here. I don't forget things like that. I'm loyal to a fault. In all my time running with my crew and working for my boss I never flipped, not once. Hell, I spent ten years in the can because of my loyalty, so don't worry, you'll get a call soon."

Yeah, sure he would. I rolled my eyes.

Harry, Jimmy, and I chatted for a while and talked shop. Jimmy finally stood up and said we had to go back to the hotel and wait for a call from the agent.

"Let me drive you back," Harry offered.

"That's OK, we'll just take a cab."

"You're in my town; please let me give you a ride. My truck has plenty of space."

Jimmy finally agreed. As Harry went around the corner to get his truck, I asked Jimmy, "Who am I meeting today?"

"It's a surprise, kid. Be patient."

Just then Harry pulled up with his truck, a 1970's open-air Bronco. The seats were held together with duct tape. It was amazing. I jumped in, but Jimmy was already having issues just getting into the truck. I sat up front, and Jimmy managed to get into the back seat.

"Sorry about the dog hairs, Jimmy. My babies love to sit in the back."

Jimmy looked down, and his black pants were covered in white dog hair. I was loving every minute of this.

"Everyone strap in. My shocks aren't what they used to be."

With that, Harry took off down the street. It was like riding a busted-down roller coaster. We felt every bump, pothole, and nuance of the road. I was having a ball, but when I looked back at Jimmy I was in heaven.

Jimmy's face was pale, kind of like when he flew. He was holding on for dear life. All the blood had left his hands as he gripped the roll bar.

"Jimmy, you OK?" I asked.

Jimmy muttered something, but with the wind blaring by and the noise of the street, I couldn't hear a thing. He wasn't happy. With every bump it looked like he was about to fall out of the truck.

Harry was blasting his rock music as we darted through L.A. traffic. I did love seeing Jimmy suffer a bit. When Jimmy was put in situations like that, where he couldn't put on the badass mobster persona, he turned back into a human being. In his mind he was just trying to survive the trip. It was glorious.

Harry pulled up to our hotel and dropped us off. I thanked him for the ride and helped Jimmy out of the back. He was white as a ghost, covered in dog fur, and his hair was everywhere. He looked like Doc Brown from *Back to the Future*.

"Call me when you have my part ready," said Harry. "Best of luck. See you boys on the flip side."

He took off into the L.A. traffic like Don Quixote. God, I had missed Harry. He was amazing to hang out with. I just loved his energy. I really hoped that Jimmy could get this film off the ground. I'd love to work with him again.

THE HOLLYWOOD KID

After that amazing car trip with Harry, Jimmy got a phone call. He told me he set up a lunch appointment with a big-time actor who was interested in the project.

"Why didn't you tell me about this sooner, Jimmy?"

Still trying to catch his breath and wipe the dog hair off his pants, he said, "Don't worry about it. This actor wants to meet with the director alone . . . so don't fuck it up."

"Who is it?"

"It's Johnny Hollywood."

Holy crap, Johnny Hollywood! I'd followed Johnny's career since he was a child star. He'd been working in Hollywood for decades. Never really had a breakout role, but recently played a villain in a big blockbuster that finally put him on the map.

Jimmy set up the meeting at The Ivy, one of the poshest restaurants in Beverly Hills where actors go to be seen.

As I was being dropped off by my cab, I saw a gaggle of paparazzi snapping photos of everyone who walked in and out of the restaurant. I strutted up to the entrance preparing myself for the onslaught of flashbulbs, but of course, they all ignored me. To be honest, it was a much-needed hit to my already-inflated ego.

I was seated at a corner table and waited. Thirty minutes passed and no Johnny Hollywood. Was he coming? Did Jimmy screw up again and threaten his agent? Just when I thought I was going to eat lunch alone I saw a flurry of lightbulbs out front by the entrance. Johnny Hollywood had arrived.

He was dressed in Hollywood chic—torn jeans, cowboy boots, a worn t-shirt, and a blazer. The outfit looked as though he had gotten it at a thrift store, but I was sure it cost a fortune. He put out his cigarette and introduced himself.

The conversation started quickly. I expressed how I was a fan of his work, which always helps when speaking to an actor, and how I watched all of his films while I worked at the video store. He thanked me, but seemed a bit disinterested. From the moment we began to speak I could feel an arrogance coming from his side of the table. An arrogance that could only come from a person raised in Hollywood.

As the lunch continued, he asked me about the project, how I got involved, and if Jimmy was the real deal. The only time I saw Johnny perk up and listen to me was when I was talking about Jimmy. Why is it that all actors are fascinated by mobsters?

Johnny started to grill me a bit about experience and how I planned to shoot the film. I'd had nothing but time to think about how to respond to this kind of question over the course of the last few months with Boris, so I was prepared. I spouted off ideas for cameras and lenses I planned to use and listed films I was inspired by. I could see Johnny's eyes glaze over. His cell phone rang, and he picked it up as I was in mid-sentence.

This guy was an arrogant little prick. It was the first time I met someone from young Hollywood. The other actors were old school, but this guy was just an ass.

When he got off the phone, he gave a great performance and said, "Listen, Alex, I have to go, but this project sounds amazing. I'd love to be a part of it. Have Jimmy call my agent and we'll work out the details. I've gotta run back to the studio to do some ADR. Later."

Before I could even respond Johnny Hollywood was gone into a sea of paparazzi flashbulbs. I'm sure Johnny delivered that same line a million times before. Of course, I was left to pay the bill. Seventy-eight dollars for an appetizer and a couple of drinks, that seemed fair.

IS THAT A REVENGE OF THE JEDI POSTER?

After I got back to the hotel, Jimmy grilled me on the meeting. "How did it go, kid? Do we have him locked in?"

"I don't know. He seemed like he was interested. He told me to tell you to call his agent and start talking money."

"Really? Holy shit, kid, if we get Johnny Hollywood in this film, people will be begging me to take their money."

At that point I didn't want to tell him what I really thought of Johnny Hollywood. I learned how full of crap most people were in this town, and just because someone said something didn't mean they actually meant it, so I let Jimmy have his moment. He told me we were heading over to Bobby and Shane's offices in West Hollywood.

The taxi dropped us off in front of a large, old office building. As we walked, we could tell this place was a bit run down. We entered the elevator and pressed six. The clanking and grinding as the doors closed was a bit unsettling.

We finally got up to the sixth floor. The halls looked like something I used to see going to my childhood dentist's office in the '80s. I found Bobby and Shane's office. I was expecting something a bit higher-end, but these guys were still young and coming-up in the business. This is just how it goes. In Hollywood you put out an image for everyone and the truth is rarely seen. Even though their offices weren't million-dollars stunning, they were making moves in the business.

There was a huge projection television running dailies from their latest film, starring Vin Diesel, playing in the background while people worked away at their desks. Bobby walked up to us.

"Welcome to our humble offices, guys."

I looked at the wall, and hanging there was an incredibly rare original *Revenge of the Jedi* poster. George Lucas pulled the original *Return of the Jedi* title two weeks before its release, and those "Revenge" posters are worth a small fortune.

"Is that an original *Revenge of the Jedi* poster?"

"Good eye, Alex. Yes, it is," Bobby told us. "Cost me a bunch, but it's worth it."

Jimmy didn't understand one thing we were saying. Bobby pulled us into his conference room, and we sat down.

"Shane is on-set with Vin dealing with drama, but he sends his best," said Bobby. "So, Jimmy, we've been working on seeing who we can attach to this film. We have investors lined up once we have a cast in place. Any luck with Johnny Hollywood?"

"The kid met with him, and things are looking good. I'll call his agent when we get back home. Don't want to look too fucking desperate."

"That's great. If you need us to come in and help, let us know."

I don't know why Jimmy didn't let Bobby and Shane help more. They could be making the phone calls and talking to agents. Jimmy's ego just wouldn't have it. He'd lose his shit if he didn't feel he was in one hundred percent control of every aspect of the project.

He brought that mentality from his days in the mob. When you are running a crew, you always have to be in total control or you might get whacked. But the film business is a team effort. You can't do it all by yourself. You need to gather a group of people with skills you do not have and let them do what they do. Jimmy had an extremely hard time with that.

"We have to head out, Bobby."

"Do you guys want to grab dinner on the set with Vin?"

"Can't do it. We have a flight back east in a couple of hours." And with that, we said our goodbyes. Another trip to La La Land was coming to a close. Who knew if we were any closer to making this godforsaken film. I was just along for the ride.

I'd miss Los Angeles. Little did I know that it would be a while before I'd get back to the city of broken dreams. L.A. has an energy that is hard to explain. It's not the prettiest city in the world, but it grows on you, and before you know it, you can't live without it.

When Jimmy and I finally got home he had a surprise waiting for me, and not a pleasant one.

CHAPTER 13

It's All Going to Be Fine, I Swear!

First day back in the office, I was swamped by the team. Everyone wanted to know what happened and if we had a star or money attached to the project yet. There was a desperation in the air.

The team wanted to get started already. It had been months for some and years for others in the office. Every time I'd travel to Los Angeles with Jimmy it was like I was their lifeline. Before I could say a word, Jimmy marched in as if he were returning a conqueror.

"Did I make it happen or what?"

The team was excited with anticipation. Was this film finally a go?

"Me and the kid had a fucking great trip. We met a few actors, some money people, and one of the biggest directors in Hollywood. Isn't that right, kid?"

I just nodded my head.

"We should have some money drop any day now."

A cheer rang out in the room. The only two not cheering were Frank and Boris.

"So get back to work because we have an Oscar-winning movie to make."

Jimmy left, and Boris and Frank pulled me into my office.

"OK, Alex, what really happened?"

"Are we actually going to start shooting?" asked Boris

I told them everything. From not meeting the actor from *Friends* because of his grandmother's passing, to Jimmy yelling in an In-N-Out parking lot, and seeing one of the biggest directors in Hollywood piss his pants when Jimmy said hi.

"A lot of potential, but nothing solid, guys."

Boris and Frank were deflated, as was I.

ENTER THE WEASEL

A few days later Jimmy called me into his office. Being called into his office was like playing Russian roulette: you never knew when the bullet was going to come. Some days he would be funny and kind, like Joe Pesci from *Goodfellas,* but then the next moment he might blow up and say, "Am I a clown? What's so funny about me?" You just never knew. I walked in and sat down.

"Listen, kid, I've been getting back a lot of feedback from people in Hollywood about the script. You did a good job with the rewrite, but I think we need to get a professional script doctor involved."

I thought to myself, *Yes, Jimmy, the script is the problem. Or could it possibly be that every time you don't get your way you threaten to kill the agent or manager on the phone?*

"So I reached out to some connections, and I have a screenwriter flying in tomorrow from Los Angeles to script doctor the fuck out of it."

I wasn't really that offended, considering I didn't even have my name on the screenplay to begin with, even though I changed the majority of it.

"That sounds great, Jimmy. Who is this guy?"

"He's one of the top script doctors in Hollywood. You know me, I only get the best. He'll be with us for a few weeks doing the polish on the script."

A few weeks? That was wishful thinking. As Boris always said, "You can check in to Hotel Jimmy, but you can never check out."

The next day I headed over to the hotel to meet the script doctor, Mark. Jimmy introduced me to him, and he sized me up instantly. He was dressed in Hollywood's uniform: t-shirt, blazer, jeans, and, of course, cowboy boots.

Mark had what I like to call "L.A. slick" dripping off of him. The guy who acts like he's a Hollywood mover and shaker but who is really waiting tables at a bistro in West Hollywood. I didn't see as clearly then, but now, living in Los Angeles for as long as I have, I can spot it a mile away.

In my experience, the guy who's talking a lot about making a film or doing something big generally isn't doing anything. People who are actually doing something are too busy doing it to talk about it.

"So glad to meet you," said Mark. "I heard nothing but good things about you from Jimmy here."

"Same here, Mark."

"I was just talking to Bruce the other day about young up-and-coming filmmakers and what they are doing with today's technology."

"Bruce?"

"Bruce Willis. I worked with him on something years ago."

See what I mean?

Like all things Jimmy, Mark had a deadline, a fake deadline, of course, that Jimmy pulled out of his ass. Apparently, Mark needed to rewrite the entire script in five days. For those of you reading this who are not familiar with the screenwriting process, five days for a full rewrite of a screenplay is *insane*!

Mark seemed to be up to the challenge. He was really trying to impress Jimmy. This guy had no idea who he had just gotten into bed with.

Jimmy set him up in a nice hotel. I had no idea where the money was coming from, but that was Jimmy's thing—impress them up front, then slowly get them into the web, and by the time they see things have changed they are already trapped.

Mark literally locked himself in his hotel room for five days straight. The room-service bill must've been insane. He spoke to no one during that time, other than to do a four-hour interview with Jimmy on day one. Jimmy loved that. Anytime he could talk about himself he was happy.

On the morning of day six, Jimmy and I went to Mark's hotel room. We knocked, and the man who opened the door didn't look like the person I met five days earlier. Mark looked like he had been through hell. He had permanent bed head, there were food plates everywhere, and the smell in the room was, let's say, not pleasant. Whether that was for real or a performance for Jimmy I'll never know.

"Here you go. It wasn't easy, but I think I cracked it," said Mark, and handed both of us a copy of the new script.

"This fucking guy. I can't believe you actually did it."

"I haven't slept in days, so if you guys don't mind, I'd love to sleep for a few days now."

"Of course, of course. Let's let the man sleep, kid. He's earned it."

We left Mark to his slumber. While waiting for the elevator Jimmy turned to me.

"Kid, don't let anyone read this yet. I want to make sure that it's not a total train wreck."

"Not a problem, Jimmy."

I went home that night, sat down on my couch, which was covered with past-due credit card bills, and started to read Mark's opus. As I went through the new script, I couldn't help but notice what a love fest it had become. The entire script was a love letter to Jimmy's ego.

Mark pulled out much of my rewrite that made the film more raw and real. Instead, what we got was an embarrassing and unrealistic version of Jimmy's life. Hell, he looked like a damn hero in this script. He even added in the ridiculous Star Trek ending that Jimmy had in twenty drafts earlier. I already knew what Jimmy was going to think.

"I fucking love this script!"

When I got into the office the next day Jimmy had Sam make copy after copy of the screenplay.

"This guy really got me. It's the closest thing to actually living my life. Fucking love it. Kid, what do you think, am I right or what?"

"Oh yeah, you were right."

"Goddamn right I was!"

The script started to circulate around the track. I went upstairs to my office, and Boris had already read the entire script. He pulled me aside. "My friend, this script is a blowjob to Jimmy's ego."

"I know, I know."

"We can't shoot this!" Boris exclaimed.

"I agree, but I can only fight so much now. Let's see if we can actually get the money and stars to make this film, and then we'll worry about the script."

Frank came running in, and before he got a word out we shouted, "We know, we know."

"I have to reschedule the entire movie . . . again!"

Jerry, the production designer, came running in as well. "Is he fucking kidding with this? We'll have to change everything. Four months of work is mostly gone."

"Don't worry, we won't be shooting this version."

I had to talk all the department heads off the ledge. The consensus in the office was all the same—it was an ego-stroking version of the script that really wasn't that compelling. Jimmy didn't understand the amount of work it would be to go with this new version, but I had a feeling this version wouldn't see the light of day.

A few days later Mark came to the office and Jimmy introduced him to the entire team. As we walked around, I could see the lights going off in Mark's head. He'd directed a feature film a couple of years earlier, and I saw him getting the itch to direct again. I truly believe that his plan the entire time was to fly in from L.A. and size me up. He had eyes on directing this film as soon as he took the writing gig.

It was weird. I desperately wanted out of Jimmy's world, but I became protective as hell with the threat of someone else coming in and trying to take my job. Human beings are truly bizarre creatures.

Jimmy started to send this version of the script out to whatever agents and managers were still taking his calls. The response wasn't what Jimmy was hoping for. Coverage came back, and the reviews were harsh. Jimmy handled the criticism with grace. I'm kidding, of course. He lost his collective shit.

"Mutha fuckin' Hollywood bullshit. They wouldn't know a good script if it smacked them in the fuckin' face."

For a few days I stayed out of Jimmy's way. I didn't want to get hit with any shrapnel. Mark was given a pass by Jimmy for some reason. It wasn't Mark's fault; it was those "cocksuckers" in Hollywood.

Mark flew back to Los Angeles, but he really never left. He was always in Jimmy's ear. The agent who set up the deal with Mark called Jimmy at least twice a week to discuss how things were going and to see if the project was moving forward. She was constantly trying to pitch Mark as a potential new director to replace me.

For whatever reason, Jimmy never faltered. He always said he was sticking with me. Why? I have no idea. Maybe because Mark would have been more difficult to control, or maybe because Jimmy had some twisted type of loyalty to me because I'd been with him so long. It makes my brain hurt just thinking about it. For now, I'm still attached to this runaway roller coaster . . . for now.

ENTER THE TABITHA

Every once in a while, Jimmy would pull a rabbit out of his hat. There would be a new meeting with a big actor or producer, some money would drop to keep things going, or a new crew member would show up. How he pulled off what I'm about to tell you still baffles me to this day.

I got called in to Jimmy's office one day. "Kid, do you watch that cable show *Miss Big Ratings?*"

"Everyone watches that show," I told him. "It's like the biggest show on television right now."

"How would you like to work with their costume designer?"

"You mean Tabitha? She's an icon. Her style is literally changing Hollywood right now."

"Well, I got her."

I was speechless.

"She arrives tomorrow to start prepping. I think she's a lesbian like Jennie. Hey, Jennie, is Tabitha gay like you?"

Jennie gave Jimmy a nasty look.

"I guess that's a yes. From the video interviews I saw, she sounds like she smokes ten cigars a day."

Sid started doing an impression of her, and Jimmy died laughing. I won't say what was said, though, because I have respect for the real Tabitha.

Sure enough, the next day, Tabitha arrived from New York. The entire crew heard she was coming and was excited to see how Jimmy would interact with a high-powered fashion icon who was a bit outside of his comfort zone.

Jimmy played it perfectly. He was a born liar, so I'd expect nothing else. He took Tabitha on a tour of the production offices and introduced me as the director.

"It's an honor to be working with you, Tabitha," I told her truthfully.

"Thank you. When my agent pitched me the story, I knew I had to be a part of it. *Miss Big Ratings* is on hiatus for a few months, so I thought why not jump on a film to kill the time."

"The kid here will take good care of you. If you need anything, let me know."

Tabitha thanked him and got started setting up her work area. Bringing her on was a bold move on Jimmy's part. The rest of the crew knew we were nowhere close to starting this film. Once Tabitha discovered that, she would be gone. Jimmy's plan was to leverage her presence to pitch new investors and see if he could finally get this film going.

A bold gamble, to say the least, because Jimmy would probably be dead in the water if it didn't work.

Days passed, and Tabitha and I were working great together. She got along with all the other department heads. Friday came, and as the pay checks were being handed out, she noticed that not everyone was getting envelopes. She pulled Jerry aside and asked, "Why didn't you get a check?"

"Many of us have been here for months without getting a check."

She was appalled.

"What? Why don't you leave?"

"Some of us tried to leave but weren't given permission."

"*Permission?*"

Jerry gave Tabitha a look, and she understood what was going on. She came to Boris and me and pulled us into my office. She asked if it was true, and we both explained everything to her. Her New York sensibility kicked in, and she went straight down to Jimmy's office.

"Jimmy, I'm leaving tomorrow."

"Why? What happened, Tabitha?"

"You have people working here who haven't been paid in months. I do not work on productions like this. Give me the money that is owed to me, and get me on a flight back to New York tomorrow. I am out of here."

Jimmy was a bit flustered because he couldn't react in his normal threatening manner. It would be over if word got back to Hollywood that Jimmy threatened a legend like Tabitha. In a move that no one saw coming, Jimmy agreed to do everything she asked. As she took her check and was walking out, she said, "And pay these people the money they are fucking owed."

She slammed the door behind her. Sid, Sam, and Jennie were in the room, and trust me, they wished they weren't. Jimmy's face turned fifteen shades of red. He yanked me into his office.

"Who the fuck flipped on me? Who turned colors? These mutha fuckers. I'm killing myself to get this movie made, and all those cocksuckers are whining about a few missing paychecks. I've lost millions of dollars and fifteen years of my life trying to make this film. Who's going to pay me back? Who? Now we lost Tabitha because someone snitched. If something like this ever happens again, I'm going to hold you personally responsible, kid. Do you fucking understand? Now get control of your fucking crew."

I walked out of his office shaking. The wall of stress on my shoulders was immense. I was twenty-six years old. I had no idea how to cope with this, with Jimmy. I went back to my office, locked the door, and had a full-blown panic attack. I couldn't breathe. It felt like my heart was about to burst out of my chest.

I laid down on the floor for a while and quietly attempted to meditate and calm myself down. I didn't really meditate often back then, only when I was super stressed. After about thirty minutes, the wave of panic subsided. I was able to pick myself up and leave the building without having the team see me fall apart.

As I was walking to the car, my beeper went off. It was my mother. Damn, I had completely forgotten I had to take her to a doctor appointment.

I haven't spoken about my parents a lot in this book because they really didn't know how to help me through this experience I was going through. They divorced when I was very young, but I always had both of them in my life. My father was a blue-collar guy who had little understanding of what the film business was, or even what I did, and my mother was going through some health issues at the time and really didn't have the bandwidth to help me. I honestly don't think she could've done much even if she had tried.

I picked her up and took her to the appointment. When we were done, we walked back to my car and I burst out crying as I sat in the driver's seat. I couldn't hold it in anymore. The stress and pressure finally broke me. It only took seven months.

Mom was completely confused. She thought I was crying about her medical issues. I told her everything that was happening to me. As I knew, she really had no way of helping other than consoling me.

I sat in that car sobbing for thirty minutes, just unleashing every-thing. I was like a pressure cooker that just exploded. Thank God I was young and didn't have a heart condition, because this would have been the heart-attack moment for me.

I drove my mother back to her house and went home. When I got to my place I just went to the shower, turned on the water, and sat in the tub weeping. I couldn't take this anymore. I felt so trapped, like a prisoner of my own dream.

In my head I blamed everyone but myself. I was the one who had to leave this situation, but I just didn't have it in me. I was burnt out. I really didn't know how I was going to go on. If I left, then I would fear for my life. Jimmy told everyone they would be looking over their shoulders for the rest of their lives if they crossed him.

So, if I left, I was dead. If I stayed, I was being killed little by little, day by day. I really had nowhere to turn. I had no one I could really talk to or turn to for help. As they say, I was screwed either way I went.

THE JENNIE INCIDENT

Jennie had been Jimmy's assistant for a few months now. She had the unfortunate job of being the closest to Jimmy on the production. Jennie had a front-row seat to all things Jimmy. Jimmy, of course, would bust her balls about being gay on a daily basis.

What I found wonderful about Jennie was that she would give as much as she got. If Jimmy made some stupid remark about her, she would hit him back with one of her own. Jimmy loved that. He would push her just to see what she would do. Jennie never disappointed.

She ran a tight front office. Since Jimmy had an allergic reaction whenever he touched a computer, Jennie handled all of that for him.

One day Jennie overheard that Sam was putting all of the office expenses on his credit cards. She asked Sam if that was true, and he confirmed it. She flipped out. I think the pressure of working so close to Jimmy finally got to her.

She went right to Jimmy and confronted him about this in front of the entire front office. If you corner a wild dog, it will come out fighting, and Jimmy was no exception.

"Who the hell do you think you are, Jennie?"

"I'm the one who keeps your bullshit production running, that's who."

Boris and I walked in right as this was going on. Jimmy's eyes started to twitch, and he turned to look at us.

"This fucking broad. I give her a job, pull her off the streets, and this is my payment."

"Off the streets? What the fuck? I'm not some whore you pulled in from a strip club, Jimmy. I'm tired of you abusing me and all of these amazing people. Why do you have Sam paying your fucking bills? Aren't you man enough to pay your own bills?"

Jennie knew that Jimmy wouldn't lift a finger against her because she was a woman. Jimmy still lived by a code—no women, no children. We all hoped he stilled lived by that code. She was able to talk to Jimmy in the way we all wish we could. Jimmy exploded.

"GET THE FUCK OUT OF MY OFFICE, YOU CUNT! YOU'RE FIRED!"

"I'm not fired, Jimmy. I just quit!"

She grabbed her things and took off. As she walked out, she had a *Jerry Maguire* moment and left us all with some parting words.

"You guys need to stop being pushed around and bullied by this fucking guy. He's not going to do a thing to you. Fight back!"

"GET THE FUCK OUT OF HERE, JENNIE!"

"Or what, Jimmy, are you going to whack me? Fuck you, Jimmy."

She walked out. In all the time we'd been on the project we had never seen anyone talk to Jimmy like that. I don't think Jimmy had ever been spoken to that way before. Like roaches when you turn on the lights, everyone scattered. Jimmy paced in the office like a caged tiger. I went back upstairs with Boris.

I would like to say that Jennie was alright and that nothing happened to her, that she lived a good life, and Jimmy never bothered her again but . . . I'm just kidding, she's fine. Jimmy never touched her. Her film-business itch had most definitely been scratched, and she left the business for good. She moved out of state and went back to school to become a nurse.

You would think something changed after that, but nothing did. Everyone was still trapped at Hotel Jimmy, where you could check in, but you could never check out. Jennie did, however, prove that you could check out, and the first chink in Jimmy's armor had been revealed. Maybe there was hope for the rest of us.

CHAPTER 14

Worst Day in American History

I was driving to the production office, listening to Howard Stern on the radio. I was dreading my day, as I usually was, but then I heard Howard start talking about a plane hitting the World Trade Center. I was just parking at the racetrack when he started talking about the incident.

I ran inside, and everyone was gathered around the television. The worst day in American history was unfolding in front of our eyes. People in my crew were shocked; some were crying. Jimmy walked in and yelled out, "What is everyone doing? Are we making a movie here or what?"

Then he saw what was happening on the television. For a moment Jimmy was quiet. We all sat and watched the horrors of that day. Jimmy, of course, eventually had to make 9/11 about himself.

"My family helped build the twin towers. It was made by Italians. I've got pictures somewhere of my uncles building it."

How could Jimmy be so self-centered at a moment like this? He couldn't stand not being the center of attention. When he saw that no one was paying any attention to him he left.

Once the paranoia started to set in, my crew started to look to me for answers. *Are we safe here? Should we all go home?* I made a decision to let the crew go home and be with their families until we all, as a nation, figured out what just happened. The world was going nuts, and there was no way anyone would be able to work.

The crew left, and I jumped on the elevator to go home as well. On the way down, it stopped at Jimmy's floor. When the doors opened, I found an extremely pissed-off Jimmy.

"Who the fuck gave you permission to release the crew? Who, mother fucker, who? I'm the captain of this ship!"

I mumbled my answer and he said, "What? What did you say, you little cocksucker?"

I just put my head down to avoid eye contact so as not to anger the psychotic grizzly any further.

"That's what I thought! Don't ever cross me again, kid. Don't take my kindness for weakness. I will still bust your fucking head wide open and dump you in a ditch. Get the fuck out of here."

What was this psycho talking about? I didn't cross him. I was just helping my crew deal with what had just happened to our nation. We were all scared and confused. The first few days of 9/11 were a scary time. No one knew what the hell was going on. Jimmy could only think of himself and his ego.

I left shaking like a leaf, again. When I got home, I sat and watched CNN for five days straight. We didn't go back to work for a week. No one could work anyway. Jimmy reluctantly agreed.

ANOTHER ESCAPE ATTEMPT

A few weeks went by and things were getting worse and worse. My crew and I were still dealing with the aftermath of 9/11. That, along with the money that was always supposed to drop but never did, made the crew restless.

I dreaded driving into work every morning. I couldn't sleep. I had gained weight. The stress was tearing me apart. I needed to get out of this situation, or I would have a heart attack or something.

One morning I mustered up the courage to walk into Jimmy's office and sit down. This was the day, the day I was finally going to be released from my personal hell.

"Listen, Jimmy, I want to thank you for this amazing opportunity. It has been a dream come true to work on such an amazing project, but I truly believe that my attachment to this film as the director is hurting it. You can't get funding because I'm attached, and you are having problems getting any big-name actors to sign on the dotted line. I think it would be best for the film if I just bow out and let someone else take the helm."

I must have practiced that speech in the mirror at least a hundred times.

"Kid, I appreciate what you are trying to do, but you are my guy. I don't change horses midstream. You are my guy 'til the end."

My heart dropped into my shoes. I couldn't move. *Have I just been given a life sentence here? Will I never be able to leave this hell?*

"Getting the money and the actors is my job. Go back upstairs and get back to work. We have a film to make, kid. The crew needs their leader. You are my guy, don't forget that."

I nodded and walked out like someone had just killed my dog. I was chasing my dream, and that dream had been torturing me for almost a year now. What the hell was I going to do?

As I rode the elevator back up to the top floor, I started to cry. My emotions couldn't be bottled up anymore. I had no idea what I was going to do.

I went to one of the abandoned bars and sat in a dark corner. I was at the end of my rope. I had no one to turn to. Boris and Frank were my only lifelines, and they were trying to figure out how to get out as well. My life was crumbling down around me. Would this ever stop? Was this the *Twilight Zone?* Was I permanently stuck in an episode of *The Sopranos? This is not what I signed up for. God, please let me out. Put an end to this madness.* I sat in that broken-down restaurant for a few hours, contemplating what I could do to escape.

Unfortunately, I was raised in an environment that always allowed me to quit. Throughout my life, up to that point, I would quit if I was even a little uncomfortable with the situation.

So my first instinct when times got rough was to take off and leave. The universe put me in a situation that didn't allow that option. Whether you believe in karma or not, Jimmy sure felt like a boatload of it. I thought maybe I needed to deal with this in order to move on in life.

As I was contemplating why the universe put me in this horrible situation, Frank and Boris were planning their own escape.

THE GREAT ESCAPE

November rolled around, and Thanksgiving was coming up. Frank and Boris were plotting how they could get out of Dodge and see their families again. Boris came to me and told me his plan of escape. The first thought I had was, *God, please don't leave me here alone.*

After Boris laid out his plan, I wished him the best of luck. He took the death trap of an elevator down to Jimmy's office. Boris walked in and asked, "Jimmy, do you have a second to talk?"

"For you, Boris, of course."

"Listen, Jimmy, you know I love this project, and I can't wait to shoot the hell out of this movie for you, but the holidays are coming up and I haven't seen my family in a few months. I would like to go home for the holidays, and if the money drops anytime during the holidays, I will be back here the next day. I just really want to see my family."

Jimmy sat for a second and pondered what Boris just requested.

"You're not turning colors on me, Boris, are you?"

"Of course not, Jimmy. I love this project. Hell, I think it even has a shot at an Oscar. I know what this film can do for my career, so trust me, I'll be back. I just really miss my family."

"Okay, Boris, go spend time with your family. I know what it feels like to be away from your family. I spent ten years in a metal box wishing every moment of every day I was with my family. But don't take my kindness as weakness. You better not turn colors on me, Boris."

"I would never, Jimmy. Thank you very much. I'll start packing and leave tomorrow."

And with that they shook hands and it was done. Once Boris got upstairs, he told Frank and me the entire story. Part two of their plan was up next. Frank went downstairs to ask for his release papers.

"What the fuck is going on, Frank? Is everyone abandoning ship like rats?"

"Jimmy, I've been with you on this journey longer than anyone else."

"I know, I know."

"I've been attached to this project for eight years. Anytime you ask for anything I'm there. This is the closest you've ever been to making your movie, but it's the holidays, Jimmy, and I want to see my family."

"All right, Frank, you win. Go and spend time with your family. If the money drops, I'll give you a call."

"And I'll be here in a second, Jimmy. Thank you. I'll leave with Boris tomorrow."

Frank came back upstairs to my office and let me know the news. I had a sense that their meeting with Jimmy was like a parole hearing. On the outside I was very happy for them, but on the inside I was devastated. The only two anchors I had were leaving the next day.

I still remember the extreme sadness I felt as I walked Boris and Frank to their taxi.

"My friend, don't worry," said Boris. "We'll come back, but you need to start thinking about moving to Los Angeles. You're wasting your time here. Someone like you would do very well in LA."

Frank agreed with Boris 110 percent. "You need to get out of here."

"I know, but I can't wrap my head around that right now."

Then Boris said something that stuck with me for a long time: "The only thing you will regret about moving to Los Angeles is that you didn't do it sooner."

With that, all six and a half feet of Boris gave me a huge bear hug before he hopped into the taxi. Frank and I said our goodbyes, and he joined Boris. As they drove away, I knew they were never coming back. I knew I was on my own for the rest of this journey, and I was terrified.

To add insult to injury, my girlfriend and I were having troubles. The problem was that I had no idea. I don't speak a lot about my ex-girlfriend in this book because I didn't want to bring her into this, but she had a profound impact on this time of my life. She, too, had no idea how to help me deal with Jimmy. She did her best, but again, just like my parents, she simply wasn't capable.

My girlfriend did go out on a few dinners with Jimmy and heard the stories of my adventures in Hollywood. She was one of the few people I could actually talk to about the whole scenario, even if it was just to vent. In many ways, she was the last thing I had to hold on to during this difficult time in my life.

One night after we had dinner, I thought everything was going perfectly well. I asked if she wanted me to come over to her apartment, but she said she had to study. We said goodbye and I went home. Thirty minutes later, I got a call from her. She was breaking up with me. I was so involved with what was going on in my life that I didn't even have a clue that there were problems with our relationship.

I pleaded for her not to leave, but for better or worse, she did. I was completely and totally alone. I remember falling to the floor in my kitchen and curling up in the fetal position, having a full-blown meltdown a few days before Christmas.

That was probably the roughest holiday season I had ever gone through. Christmas came and went without a lot of fanfare. I was broke, heartbroken, and constantly in fear of the psychotic gangster ruling over my life. But like they say, "It's darkest just before the dawn," and a flicker of hope was right around the corner.

CHAPTER 15

Want to Meet Batman?

It had been a few weeks since Boris and Frank left. Hollywood pretty much shuts down between Thanksgiving and the second week of January. Very few deals are made, so there hadn't been much action in the office. I got a call from Jimmy the day after Christmas.

"Hey, kid, what are you doing tomorrow?"

"Not much, Jimmy. What do you have in mind?"

"Do you want to go meet Batman?"

"What?"

"Do you want to go meet Batman?"

I was so exhausted I said, "Sure, Jimmy, I'd love to meet Batman."

"Great. We leave tomorrow to go meet him at his ranch."

"Wait a minute. Are you serious? Are we actually going to meet Batman?"

Jimmy sent out the script to one of the actors who played Batman, and he loved it. Batman wanted to meet us the next day. After having such a shitty Thanksgiving and Christmas, this was extremely welcome news. Holy crap, I was going to meet Batman.

I found myself with Jimmy at the airport again. He was dressed in his usual travel wear. As we sat down, he took his pill and was off to

La La Land. As we were flying in the air going to meet Batman, I started fantasizing about how the meeting with him would go.

You must understand this is probably the biggest thing that ever happened to me. I was about to go meet a major movie star at his ranch two days after Christmas. For an ex-video-store clerk, this was a pretty huge deal.

We landed and went straight to the hotel. Jimmy gave Batman's people a call and told him we were there. Batman's assistant, Howard, told Jimmy that he would love to have dinner with us that night. I can't tell you how excited I was.

Jimmy and I had a few hours to kill before dinner, and of course, he wanted to buy Batman a gift. He couldn't show up to meet Batman without an extravagant gift. Jimmy found some extremely expensive handmade toys to give Batman's kids.

As we went back to the hotel, Jimmy got a call. Batman's assistant told Jimmy that he wouldn't be able to make it to dinner that night, but to please enjoy a dinner on him. The first thought that went through my mind was, *Here we go again. I hope we have an In-N-Out nearby so Jimmy can have a place to yell and scream.*

Of course, Jimmy took it well.

"What do you mean Batman isn't coming to dinner? We flew thousands of miles just to see him."

"I promise you Batman will see you in the morning for breakfast at his home."

After that Jimmy calmed down a bit, and we went to dinner on Batman's dime. Later that night, I sat in my room thinking about what was going to happen the next day. I had grown up watching this actor in some of the biggest films of all time, and now I might have the opportunity to direct him.

My excitement went directly to fear. Who the hell was I to direct an icon? This was the moment I started to firmly go up my own ass and get into my head. I started overthinking the entire situation. Let's just say I didn't get much sleep that night.

The next morning, Jimmy and I got into our rental car and drove to meet Batman. We drove about two hours to his ranch. When we got to the gate it was closed. Jimmy called and leaned out of the car and pressed the button to call. Eventually, we heard a voice . . . "Hello?"

"Yeah, this is Jimmy and I'm here to—"

"Mr. Batman is expecting you. Just follow the road to the main house."

The large gate slowly opened. Jimmy and I started on a drive that seemed to take forever. We later found out it was ten miles to Batman's front door from the gate. His property was over forty thousand acres of land, including mountains, rivers, and lakes.

On our trek to his house, we saw animals running free everywhere. Deer, moose, and even buffalo. Hundreds of horses ran and played in the wild. It was a beautiful but weird way to the Bat Cave. After driving for fifteen minutes, we turned a corner and there it was—this huge mansion-style estate. In must've been ten thousand square feet, if not more.

The butterflies in my stomach were working overtime. We were greeted by Howard, Batman's assistant. "Welcome to Batman's home."

"Jesus, I thought we got lost driving around this property."

"I know, it can be a little bit overwhelming the first time you come."

We walked into the house and were taken to the kitchen. A private chef was waiting there for Jimmy and me.

"Batman is in the other room and will be with us momentarily. So, please, place your orders with our good man here and he'll make you anything you want."

The private chef had every topping you could possibly imagine for him to make us our own custom omelet. The rest of the breakfast spread was massive. You could have easily fed thirty to forty people. Jimmy and I placed orders and sat down.

The view from the kitchen was magical. A window running the length of the entire wall from floor to ceiling gave us an incredible view of the landscape. Snow drifted down on the hills in the distance. A stream ran behind the house, its top layer partly frozen over.

Rivulets of water flowed from cracked patches, giving us a view of the icy water below.

As I was chomping on my custom-made omelet, I looked over and there he was—fucking Batman. And he was wearing a cardigan.

He walked into the kitchen from outside and introduced himself. Jimmy and I both got up and shook his hand.

"Mr. Batman, it is an absolute pleasure to meet you. I loved you in that movie where you played the hitman. You really captured what it's like to kill someone."

I really couldn't believe he just said that.

"Thank you, Jimmy. I worked really hard on the part, and thanks for flying all this way just to talk to me."

"Of course, you were always my first choice for this movie. This is my director, Alex Ferrari."

"Great last name, Alex. Nice to meet you."

"It's an absolute pleasure to meet you as well. I'm looking forward to hopefully working with you on this film."

I couldn't believe I was acting as professional as I was when all I wanted to do was to get the hell out.

"Was that a buffalo I saw out there?"

"Yes, I call him Miles Davis."

"You have a beautiful property."

"Thank you. I let the local Indians hunt on the property. It was their land way before I got here. Let's sit down and talk about this amazing movie you guys have."

As we sat down, Jimmy gave Batman the gift for his kids. Batman was very thankful and called his kids in to meet us. They took one look at the toys and tossed them to the ground. They ran outside and started jumping on a gigantic trampoline in the backyard.

As professional as I was trying to be, I did have to geek out a bit. I started showering him with compliments about his amazing performances. Batman humbly thanked me for the kind words. He then started telling me behind-the-scenes stories about his films.

We must've sat for an hour just talking about film, his performances, and the craft of making movies. Of course, Jimmy was quiet. He was completely out of place and had no idea about most of the things we were talking about. For as much as Jimmy said he studied the film business, he had no idea what it actually took to make a movie.

"So you liked the script?"

"I loved this script, and the trailer was pretty amazing as well. I think this would be a great character to play."

You could see the happiness dance across Jimmy's face. To be honest, I'd never seen him so happy before. Jimmy started talking about himself, the mob, his crew, and his time in jail. I sat there quietly. After they discussed the story for a while, Batman turned to me and asked, "So, what's your vision for this film?"

This was it. It was my time to shine. I went into this entire monologue about how I was going shoot the movie. I kept referring to his entire filmography, as well as classic movies, directing styles, and even some paintings I was inspired by.

Batman seemed impressed. I was in nirvana. It seemed like something out of a story. An ex-video store clerk was sitting in a huge mansion talking to Batman about making a movie while looking out across a beautiful winter landscape. Batman and I continued to discuss the film for hours, until finally he turned to me and said, "Would you like to stay tonight? We can keep talking about the movie and maybe watch a film or two to get some inspiration."

Holy shit, Batman just invited me to sleep over his house. This can't be happening.

"Yes, I think it would be an amazing idea."

I looked to Jimmy and he was not happy. I was bonding a little too much with Batman, and Jimmy's poor little ego couldn't take it.

"Thanks, Batman, but we have to get back so we can keep prepping this film."

Jesus Christ, are you kidding me, Jimmy? I said to myself. When Batman asks you to sleep over at his place you say YES!

"I can catch a later flight and meet you there tomorrow."

"No, I think you need to come with me. The team will be expecting you."

Jimmy then gave me his patented "don't fucking cross me, kid" look.

"I guess I'm going home, then."

"Too bad. Maybe next time."

Jimmy and I got up and said our goodbyes to Batman. It took everything I had inside not to ask Batman for a picture. You have to stay professional in those situations, or at least that's what I told myself.

Batman walked us out and thanked us again for coming. He seemed really excited about the project and was looking forward to making a picture with me. As Jimmy and I drove away, I was still a bit high from the entire experience. For the first time in a long time, I actually had hope this film would get made.

CHAPTER 16

What Just Happened?

It was a week or so after New Year's, and I hadn't been back to the office just yet. Jimmy and a couple of the other core guys were there, but none of the crew had come back from the holidays yet.

I was still digesting what happened a couple of weeks earlier. Being away from Jimmy gave me time to re-energize before I got back to work. I hadn't heard a word from anyone in production since I got back from my trip to see Batman.

Monday morning rolled around, and I was packing my laptop to head into the office when the phone rang.

"Hello?"

"Hey, kid. How are you holding up?"

"I'm good, Jimmy. Just getting ready to head into the office."

"Listen, kid, I've got some bad news. Batman doesn't want to work with you."

I felt like someone drop-kicked me in the stomach.

"What? I thought everything went so well."

"So did I, but apparently he was just being polite. I got a call from his agent this weekend. He told me that Batman thinks you're just too green to work with him."

"But how is that possible?"

"I don't know, kid, but I also got a call late last week from Johnny Hollywood's people. He said they loved the movie but didn't feel that he could work with you. Said you were just too inexperienced to work with him."

I was silent

"Listen, we've been trying make this happen for almost a year now, but I think it's time we part ways. I did everything I could to make this dream come true for you, but there's things that I just don't have control over."

I mumbled a few words.

"I'm really sorry about this, kid. This is just how fucking Hollywood works. Sometimes you have to play the game. I've been on this journey for fifteen years and lost millions of dollars. Anyway, Sam's going to come by later today and pick up that laptop from you. I need to get it back to the product placement people."

"Sure, Jimmy."

"You're super talented, and I'm sure you'll get your shot one day soon. Shit like this happens in Hollywood every day. Keep your head up. I'll call you if anything changes."

I was free but absolutely devastated. It's the strangest feeling to want to leave something so badly but still hold on to that thing desperately to keep you going. I sat on the floor to contemplate what just happened to me.

So many feelings were running through me: anger, relief, revenge, sadness, depression. I must have sat there in silence for an hour. My mind just could not process what happened. While I was swirling in my own vortex of confusion, I heard a knock at the door. It was Sam.

"Hey, Alex. I'm here to pick up the computer and give you this."

Sam had cleaned out my office for me and brought everything in one of those boxes you see every character ever fired from a movie pack their stuff in. I pulled the laptop out of my bag and handed it to him.

"Thanks, Alex. Listen, I'm really sorry for the way things turned out."

You could see the emotion on his face. He truly felt sorry for me.

"Not your fault, Sam."

"Here's your final check. Jimmy said not to cash it for a couple of weeks."

Of course Jimmy said not to cash it for a couple weeks. I'll be surprised if it doesn't bounce all the way back to Batman's house.

"Thanks, Sam. Give my best to everybody else at the office."

"Sure thing, Alex."

As I shut the door, I was literally closing that chapter of my life. I was finally free, but just like a bird caged for years before its owner opens the door to let him fly, I was terrified. There was a weird comfort to being involved with Jimmy and his film.

I'd had something to do every day and hadn't had to think about much else aside from prepping the movie. In many ways I was hiding. Working with Jimmy gave me permission to stop hustling. I had Jimmy out front dragging me along in search of my dream. I didn't have to do much work at all.

To be honest, for almost a year of my life, I hid behind Jimmy and his film. But my lack of courage and fortitude placed me in the deepest, darkest hole I have ever been in.

For a few weeks after Jimmy's phone call I just stayed locked up in my house. I didn't talk to anybody. The only thing I did was watch movies. Whenever I found myself in a bad place in life I would escape into movies. It's strange the one thing that's caused me so much pain and suffering is the thing I go to for comfort in dark times.

I finally called Boris and Frank to let them know what was going on. Boris told me I would be okay, but that I had to figure out a way to get to Los Angeles. Frank agreed, but how the hell was I going to find the money to go out to Los Angeles? Frank and Boris didn't know about my financial troubles. If they had, they would've never suggested I go back to Hollyweird.

So I said fuck it and did what any other red-blooded American would do in this situation—I charged it. With the little credit I had left on my credit cards, I bought a ticket to Los Angeles and asked an old college buddy if I could crash on his couch for a month.

I still had my editing to fall back on, so I went out and made sixty VHS copies of my editorial reel and dusted off my resume. I kept what I was doing quiet because I believed that, even though I left Jimmy, Jimmy had not left me. I didn't want him to know I was trying to move to Los Angeles, for some strange reason. I'm still traumatized by him.

The plan was for me to go out to Los Angeles and hand out my editorial reel and resume. I would get a job offer, leave my home, and move out to L.A., all within thirty days. Yes, to answer your question, I was an idiot. I was so lost after what I just went through that I was literally throwing up Hail Marys in the hopes that something or someone would come to my rescue.

CHAPTER 17

I'm Going back to Cali

This was my last shot. I was putting all my chips on the table. What no one knew was that I had enough money to pay my mortgage for just one more month, and if I didn't get a job on this trip, I would have to file for bankruptcy.

This would be the first time I'd been in L.A. without Jimmy to hide behind. I was on my own and trying to take the biggest leap I've ever taken in my life, while being at the weakest point mentally, physically, and spiritually I'd ever been. Doesn't seem like a good recipe for success, does it?

Once I landed at LAX, I rented a car and headed over to my friend Greg's apartment in Van Nuys. Greg and his roommate were kind enough to offer me a couch for a month, rent free. Now, I would like to say that I was nonstop hustling from the moment I landed, but that wouldn't be the truth.

I would spend my days faxing resumes to every film company in the production guide. Once I faxed twenty or so resumes, I would tell myself, *That's good for the day*, and then I'd just wait for the phone to ring, which it never did.

Every few days I would take a ride to a production company or two and leave my VHS demo reel and, again, wait for the phone to ring, which, again, it never did.

My days were mostly spent playing PlayStation and watching movies while Greg and his roommate were at work. I ate a ton of fast food and frozen dinners. I must've gained twenty pounds while I was in L.A.

I met with Boris. We had coffee a few times, and he gave me advice on what to do while in Los Angeles. Boris was a cinematographer and didn't have any connections in editorial work. I did try to reach out to some commercial production houses in Los Angeles, but I couldn't even get through the front door.

Frank invited me to dinner at his home. When I drove up, I was taken aback by how beautiful his home was. He purchased his house in the '80s when the prices were a bit more reasonable. After dinner, we would sit on his amazing deck overlooking the twinkling lights of Los Angeles, and he would tell me stories of all the amazing people he worked with in his career.

He even connected me with his son, James, who was a post-production supervisor over at Paramount Studios. James offered me grunt editorial work, which is basically editing behind-the-scenes footage for DVD releases. I thanked them, but it just wasn't enough money for me to move out to Los Angeles. I needed a better-paying job.

One thing I didn't understand was that you can't do what I did when you try to move out to Los Angeles for the first time. It takes a while to get an opportunity or have a door open for you. If you are going to try to move out to Los Angeles, you should have at least one year of living expenses saved up. When you are starting out you have to work for free or cheap to get your foot in the door. I was under the delusion that I could get it all done within thirty days.

To add insult to injury, I got a bunch of parking tickets while I was staying at Greg's. That's something no one tells you about L.A.; they weren't cheap tickets.

I tried to reach out to the producers and people I met on my trips with Jimmy, but I never got a call back. On the last day I was in L.A. I got a call from a production company that saw my reel. They wanted to hire me as an editor for their travel videos, mostly cruise-line shows. I told them I was interested, but I was leaving to go back home and needed to pack and move back. The company said, "Thanks anyway, but we need someone to start next week."

I felt like this was Los Angeles giving me a punch in the face on the way out the door. It's fair to say that I got my ass seriously kicked by L.A. I bet the farm and lost. I just wasn't ready to take on that challenge. I was barely functioning. Now I was on my way back home, worse off than when I came. Broken, depressed, and in serious financial trouble. Isn't show business glamorous?

CHAPTER 18

Old Ghosts

I always wanted to be the kind of person who writes in a journal so that I could look back years later and see what I was thinking then. During this entire journey in my life, I unfortunately didn't write much down. I did fill up a small notebook with details for this book back then, knowing I would do something with this crazy story one day.

But I was recently cleaning out a closet when I came across a familiar notebook. It was my attempt to journal a few months after I left the film project. When I read it, I knew I had to include it in this book. It's completely raw, uncensored, and a true glimpse into how I was still dealing with what happened with Jimmy.

I have grand ideas and goals but lack the courage to proceed. My natural talent is better than many in the world, but my fear and demons have prevented me from moving forward. What I fear has been slowly revealing itself to me over the years. Only recently have I been looking for an answer. I realized that if you ask a question long enough, the answer presents itself.

How serious are you, Alex? What are you willing to do to make your dream come true? Your dream will not come knocking at your door. Right now, you should be in Hollywood making feature films for a living. Follow your path. Your choices, good or bad, have led you to this point. Are you going to finally do what you are meant to do, or are you going to waste this life?

YOU ARE A FUCKING LAZY ASS! I love you, man, but you have to get serious. You are almost thirty years old. IT'S TIME! Tomorrow you will wake up and you'll be fifty years old, angry and bitter because you didn't follow your dream, because you didn't make it happen. You'll probably be married to some sweet girl who has supported your cowardice for years. FIGHT, DAMN YOU, FIGHT! You want to have kids someday, right? How the hell can you preach to them to follow their dreams when you don't have the courage to do it yourself?

What you went through with Jimmy is just one of many beatings life will continue to give you until you learn, until you begin to show me and the universe who the FUCK the real Alex truly is. You need to try EVERY FUCKING day to move forward, even if it's just an inch a day.

I was in a dark, dark place in my life after my misadventures with Jimmy. My finances were in shambles, I had gained a ton of weight, my girlfriend had left me, and I was broke.

To hide from the world, I started selling comic books on eBay with a friend. I would hide in his garage sorting comic books for hours and hours. I would spend days, weeks, in that garage just losing myself in sorting thousands of comics. The money that trickled in from the sales of the comics would keep me fed, the lights on, and the creditors at bay, but it definitely wasn't enough to live on. After almost a year, my credit cards had run out, my checking account was near empty, and I couldn't borrow any more money.

Bankruptcy seemed my only way out. I didn't want to file for Chapter 11, but I had few options. Members of my family filed before, so I started looking into the process.

A few days before I was going to sign the paperwork, I sat in the middle of my living room and yelled out to the universe, "Listen, I don't want to do this. I want to pay my debts. I'm not that kind of person, but I have no other choice here. So, if you want me to do the right thing, I need your help. Send me some help, or I'll have no choice but to sign the bankruptcy paperwork."

As crazy as this might sound, the next morning I got a phone call from someone I hadn't heard from in years—my first boss from the commercial production company I interned at. He told me there was a job opening for an editor at a local television station. He said I should apply, that he would put in a good word for me.

I grabbed my VHS demo reel and resume and jumped in my car. I met with the producer at the station and tried to act cool during the interview. He popped in my reel and watched it.

"It's very impressive, Alex," said the producer. "I think you are the guy we've been looking for. When can you start?"

No words can express the joy and excitement I felt when I heard those words.

"Tomorrow if you like."

And with that, I was back, baby! So grateful for the opportunity. The funny thing is that the pre-Jimmy Alex would've never even considered doing this kind of work. My ego wouldn't have allowed it because, of course, I was going to be the next big Hollywood director, but the post-Jimmy Alex was not only willing but thankful for the opportunity.

Within a few months I became a full-time editor at the company. I even started doing freelance gigs on the side for extra money. I was a man on a mission. The bankruptcy papers I was about to sign were thrown in the garbage. My debts were being paid off, and I was getting back on my feet. A year later, I was able to quit my job and open my first post-production company—Numb Robot.

With Numb Robot I worked with many other filmmakers editing and color grading feature films, shorts, TV shows, music videos, and commercials. I even directed a few commercials. The universe opens doors when you need them and closes them when it knows you shouldn't go through them. It's funny how things work out.

CHAPTER 19

Can't Keep a Good Gangster Down

A 35 mm film negative was running back and forth in a telecine machine. I was color grading a commercial I just shot for a client. The colorist was running the film back and forth looking for a shot the client wanted to see again. Oddly enough, it was the same post house I met Jimmy at all those years ago.

My cell phone rang. I excused myself from the dark room. When I got into the hall I looked down at the phone and didn't recognize the number, but I answered it anyway.

"Hello?"

"Hey, kid, when are you going to direct my movie?"

My face went white and my stomach dropped to the floor. It was Jimmy. I hadn't heard from him in over three years.

"Jimmy?"

"You haven't forgotten about me already, have you? Now that you're a big-time director."

The sound of his voice triggered something in me. I was back at the damn racetrack again.

"Never, Jimmy. How could I ever forget you? How are things?"

"You know, still out here trying to get this movie made. Fucking

Hollywood pricks are always yanking my chain. They've taken me for one hell of a ride these last eighteen years. I can't tell you how many millions of dollars I've lost on this fucking movie."

As he was talking, I realized what a thrill Jimmy used to get by calling people he'd fucked over in the past. He'd never talk about the truth of what happened. He would just look for sympathy for how Hollywood had screwed him. I was in the room when he made these calls in the past. Holy crap, I was getting one of these phone calls.

"It isn't easy, Jimmy. I know. Listen, I have to run. I have a client waiting."

"Of course, of course. You're big-time now. When you make it to Hollywood don't forget me. I might call you in a few years to see if you can finance my movie."

"Gotta run, Jimmy. I'll talk to you later."

That was the last time I spoke to Jimmy. I kept an eye on his progress, or lack thereof, for a few years to come. Mostly out of curiosity rather than anything else. I read in the trades and heard through the grapevine that there was a rotating door of directors.

Over the years, I heard Jimmy suckered other directors onto his project. The players changed a bit, but the game was the same. He never got closer to making his film than when Boris, Frank, and I were on the project.

I would see Jimmy pop up on talk shows, in national magazines, and even on the radio from time to time. He would be telling his story, and I would listen. I swear attention was his lifeblood.

BORIS'S REVENGE

I kept in touch with Boris over the years. He was moving up the DP ladder in Los Angeles, while I was directing commercials and building up my post-production company. Every time I spoke to him, he would ask me, "When are you moving out to Los Angeles, my friend?"

My answer would always be, "Soon."

To be honest, it took me seven years to build up the courage to finally make the big move. One day I got a call from Boris out of the blue. He went on to tell me that he read in the *Hollywood Reporter* that Jimmy just attached an Oscar-winning actor to his film and a new director attached as well.

The kicker was that Boris was good friends with the director. When he read this story, he called up the director immediately. Boris told his friend all about Jimmy and his fiasco of a film. The director said he was meeting with Jimmy the next day.

Don't forget that Boris was still owed thousands of dollars in back pay for all the work he did while checked into Hotel Jimmy. Boris asked his friend if he could show up unannounced at the meeting. Of course, his friend said yes.

The next day Boris was sitting in the director's office with his friend when Jimmy walked in. Boris told me that Jimmy looked like he'd seen a ghost when he saw him. Boris stood up and shook his hand. "Jimmy, long time, my friend."

It took Jimmy a second to snap back into the Jimmy we knew and despised.

"Boris, how the hell are you?"

"Good, good. I hear you are interested in signing my friend here to be your new director."

"Yeah, is he any good?"

Jimmy started to laugh with his cigar-ridden voice. Boris and his friend laughed as well.

Boris stood up. "Well, I'll leave you two to your meeting. Before I go, I would love to throw my hat in the ring as a potential cinematographer for your film. I have so much invested in the project already. I would love to see it finally get made."

"Of course, Boris. You've always been my number-one guy. I can't even see this film being shot by anyone else."

Boris said his goodbyes and left. That director friend of Boris's never signed on to the film, and of course, Boris never heard from Jimmy again. Months later, Boris and I read in *Variety* that the Oscar-winner left the project citing "creative differences."

After that, Jimmy was pretty much dead in the water. No one in Hollywood would take or return his calls. I heard he crawled back to his racetrack and continued trying to get his movie off the ground again for years.

Jimmy suffered from something I witnessed in many people in the business. They get attached to a project or film and keep trying to get that one project made, no matter what, for years. If they stop trying to make this one movie, they lose all purpose in life. They get in so deep that they can't see their life without the struggle of trying to make the film.

Jimmy had nothing else going on in his life besides trying to get this movie made. He was an ex-con, so not many people were going to hire him. He had to have something to keep him busy for all those years. In many ways, I believe that Jimmy never even wanted to get his film made. He just wanted something to do. He wanted to feel important again, just like he did back in the day when he was running his crew for the mob.

CHAPTER 20

The Aftermath

After I got back on my feet, it took four years before I could direct anything other than commercials. I finally got back in the director's chair in 2005 for a short little film I made called *Broken*. That film went on to play in over two hundred international film festivals around the world and even got reviewed by the legendary film critic Roger Ebert. I also went on a mini misadventure with Hollywood on that project, but that's a story for another book.

I decided to create an over three-hour-long behind-the-scenes film about how I made *Broken* with everyday gear and packaged it with the film on DVD. I sold thousands of units while packing those DVDs out of my bedroom. I sold it straight to filmmakers who were interested in how I was able to make an action movie with over a hundred visual effects for just under $8,000.

This was the first time I attempted to share knowledge with my community. Little did I know it would take me ten years to continue what I started back then. In 2015, I launched indiefilmhustle.com, a website, podcast, and YouTube channel dedicated to helping filmmakers and screenwriters survive and thrive in the film industry. That little website has grown much bigger than I ever imagined it could. In my efforts to continue to serve my community, I launched indiefilm-hustle.tv (Indie Film Hustle TV), the world's first streaming service dedicated to filmmakers, screenwriters, content creators, and artists. Think Netflix for the creative community.

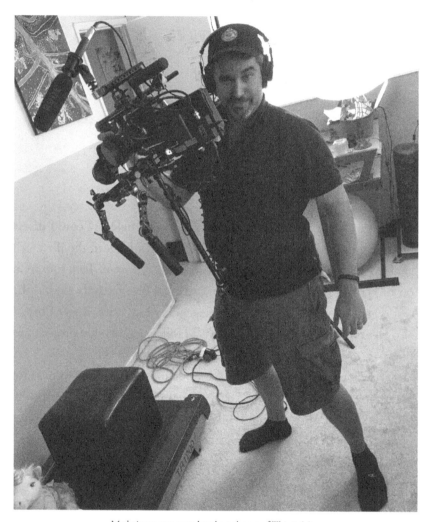

Me being a one-man-band on the set of This is Meg

Doors and opportunities started to open up for me, but only after I started to be of service to the community. Since then I've directed two feature films—*This Is Meg*, a story about an actress/comedian trying to make it in Hollywood, and *On the Corner of Ego and Desire*, my love letter to the Sundance Film Festival, Park City, and indie filmmakers. The film is a satire about three hapless filmmakers stalking a poor producer during the Sundance Film Festival and trying to sell their ridiculous independent film, all in twenty-four hours. Think *This Is Spinal Tap* for indie filmmakers.

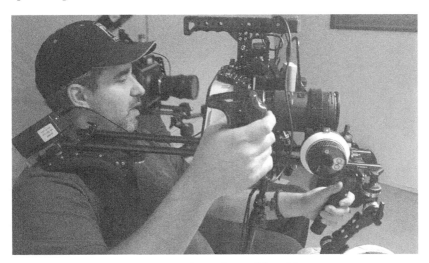

Me lining up a shot on the set of This is Meg

I've had the opportunity to direct music videos, commercials, television shows, and series shows. I never gave up chasing my dreams. Hell, I'm still chasing them now, but I'm just a little bit wiser on how to go about it.

When I met Jimmy, my dream was to be one of the biggest film directors in the world. Now I'm happy making films that are important to me and sharing my knowledge with other filmmakers, screenwriters, and artists.

Don't get me wrong, if I ever get the opportunity to make a big-budget film I will welcome it with open arms. The difference is that I'm keeping busy doing what I want to do and being happy while I'm waiting for those opportunities to arrive. That took me a long time to learn. I hope it doesn't take you as long to learn that lesson.

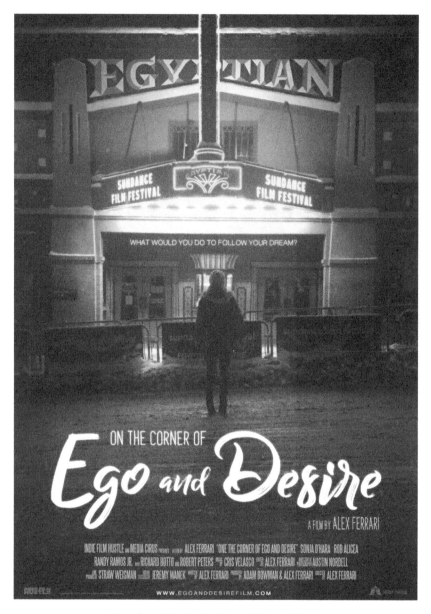

Poster for my film On the Corner of Ego and Desire

I'm still very much in touch with Boris, and he has become one of my best friends and confidantes. Boris loves to throw parties for all of his industry buddies. Anytime anyone gives him an opportunity he tells the crazy story of the gangster at the racetrack trying to make a film about his life.

Most of his friends didn't believe him and thought he was making the entire thing up, but I ended up becoming the center of attention when I moved to Los Angeles and attended some of these parties. People I didn't know would walk up to me and say, "Are you the director that Boris keeps talking about? Did it really happen? Is Jimmy a real person? Did you almost make a movie for a gangster?"

I would tell them yes, the stories were true, but then I would find myself in the middle of a small crowd. There I would weave the tale of the bipolar gangster and my misadventures in Hollyweird.

For years Boris hassled me to write the screenplay of our time spent at Hotel Jimmy. I always resisted because I didn't want to relive the darkest time in my life, and I didn't want to go and chase money or do pitches to get the film made. I wasn't going to turn into Jimmy.

One day, about a year ago, I was driving my family to the supermarket when I got a call from Boris. "Are you near a radio, my friend?" When I said that I was, he said, "Turn it to this station."

And when I turned it to that station, I heard a voice that sent shivers down my spine. It was Jimmy. I couldn't believe it. After almost seventeen years to the day, he was still at it, telling his story to anyone who would listen.

In a flash, all of it came rushing back to me. All the fear and anxiety filled me once again. I was right back at that damn racetrack all those years ago.

I pulled into the parking lot and stopped the car. I told my wife to take the kids into the store without me. She knew who it was and gave me my space. I sat there alone in my car listening to the voice of the man who brought me so much pain and suffering all those years ago. With every word he spoke I went deeper into the past. I hadn't gone to that place inside of me for easily over a decade.

When the interview was over, I sat there quietly for a minute contemplating what just happened. I reached for my phone and called Boris back. "I can't believe he's still doing it. I just can't believe it."

"My friend, you have to write the screenplay," insisted Boris.

"Boris, I'm not going to write the screenplay. Who's going to give me the money to make the movie? I don't want to go chasing money again for another film. It's a period piece about a gangster making a movie. I don't know if anybody would even care."

"Oh, trust me, they'll care. If you don't want to write the screenplay, then write a book about Hotel Jimmy."

Then I said to myself, *Damn it, I can write a book.*

"Damn you, Boris. Let me think about it."

"You won't regret it, my friend. People need to hear this story."

It was time to go back. It was time to tell my story. I didn't make the decision lightly, but I thought this story needed to be told, and hopefully other people could learn from my mistakes.

You should never stop chasing your dream. Just be guarded against people who might take advantage of you in your pursuits.

Many people along your journey will tell you they can make your dreams come true. In my twenty-five years of chasing my dream, I found that not to be the case. Working with people toward a common goal is the way to move forward. Building relationships, real relationships, with people gets you much farther and closer to your goals.

Another tip I can give you; if you're capable of it, try not to give a shit what other people think of you or your work. The second I didn't care about the good opinions of others, many of my dreams started coming true. Also, try not to attach an outcome to your art. If you do, it will stifle your work.

My final thoughts on Jimmy are that I want to thank him. Because of my experience with him, I am who I am today. That experience gave me the fuel to write this book and hopefully help someone out there not to make the same mistakes this kid did all those years ago.

Trust me, today, when someone like a Jimmy comes along my path, I see him or her coming from a mile away. It's kind of like if you have lifted a hundred-pound dumbbell all your life and one day someone hands you twenty-five pounds. Jimmy was my hundred-pound dumb-bell, and everything that came after him was a twenty-five-pound weight.

If I could meet Jimmy today, I would give him a big bear hug. Honestly, I would. As painful as that time with Jimmy was, I will be forever grateful for the experience. I wish Jimmy no ill will at all. Sometimes in life you need a trial by fire. When I met Jimmy, I was cocky, arrogant, and full of myself.

It's an ongoing effort to not let your ego interfere with your decision-making process. For most people, it's a lifelong process, and I'm not an exception to that. The experience with Jimmy was eye-opening, to say the least. It showed me how easy it is to let your ego lead you and how difficult it is to separate the ego from the self. If I could do anything over, I would make myself twenty years younger with the wisdom I have today.

Like any traumatic experience in life, it takes time to heal and recover, but at the end you are a better person for it. It's taken me close to twenty years to recover fully, and this book is my way of dealing with that time in my life.

I hope Jimmy learned something walking his path in life, because I most definitely have. Never stop following your dreams, and remember, when you meet a gangster who tells you he wants to hire you to direct a film based on his life story, just say no. That's advice I think we can all agree on.

To Anyone Chasing A Dream

You are some of the bravest souls on the planet. You have the courage to follow your dream, whatever that might be. Most people never make it that far. They talk themselves into doing something that makes them money but never truly fulfills them. You are a warrior, a dream warrior. Someone who chases what makes you happy. When you are in-line with the universe money will come. I'm a perfect example. As soon as I opened Indie Film Hustle, doors swung open for me. I started on that path back in 2005 but rejected it because of my ego. Don't let that happen to you.

Take it from someone who has been on the sometimes-difficult path of making his dream come true: it gets better. It might not be tomorrow, but it will come. When you start out you have one dream in your head that you are chasing with all your energy. Sometimes you are in-line with what the universe has in store for you, and sometimes you aren't. Understand that if your dream is coming from a pure place and not from the ego, you will get there. I promise you. It might take years or even decades, but you will get there.

Also understand that your dream may change over time. What I wanted to direct in my twenties doesn't do it for me in my forties. Be open to that change. Don't fight it. The more you fight, the more you will struggle. Be open is some of the best advice I can give you. Be open to opportunities that may not be exactly what you are looking for at the moment but that may help you along your path. You have no idea what impact following your dream will have on other people. Share with the world what is unique inside of you.

Chase your dream, but be smart about it. Take calculated risks but take risks. Take calculated chances, but take chances. You never know what will happen until you try. You may fail, but that is good. The more you fail, the more you learn. You never learn from success. Failure is the best teacher, trust me on that. Good luck to all of you dream warriors out there. Keep hustling everyday toward your goals. One step at a time is all it takes. Be well and follow that dream. What else are we here to do other than to follow the dreams that have been placed inside of our hearts?

—Alex

What's Your Story?

Once you finish reading this book I want you to share your experiences with me. If you have a story about the challenges and successes of following your dream, post it on social media. Upload pictures, text and/or videos of your journey following your dream.

Use the hashtag *#shootingforthemob* and *#ifhtribe*. Since you read this book, you are now an official member of the Indie Film Hustle Tribe. Welcome!

I'd love for you to also upload videos or pictures of you reading or listening to *Shooting for the Mob*. Follow me on social media below to stay updated on all the new podcasts, videos and content I create daily for the IFH Tribe:

Facebook: www.facebook.com/indiefilmhustle
Twitter: www.twitter.com/indiefilmhustle
Instagram: www.instagram.com/ifilmhustle
YouTube: www.indiefilmhustle.com/youtube

Indie Film Hustle Communities:

If you want to learn more about what I do daily with **Indie Film Hustle** just visit me at any of my websites:

Indie Film Hustle: www.indiefilmhustle.com
Bulletproof Screenwriting: www.bulletproofscreenwriting.tv
Filmtrepreneur: www.filmtrepreneur.com
My Official Site: www.alexferrari.com

At any of my sites you can search massive databases of inspiration, articles, knowledge, and videos on filmmaking, screenwriting, film distribution, film production and much more.

Filmmaking and Screenwriting Educational Sites:

IFH Academy:
Where filmmakers and screenwriters come to learn from industry professionals working in the business today.
www.ifhacademy.com

Indie Film Hustle TV:
Access hundreds of hours of online courses, workshops & seminars taught by some of the film industry's greatest minds. If you want to learn about screenwriting, directing actors, cameras and lenses, film distribution, or how to become a Filmtrepreneur, we have you covered.
www.indiefilmhustle.tv

Podcasts:

To provide even more value to my tribes I host a number of industry leading podcasts covering every aspect of the filmmaking and screenwriting process.

IFH Podcast: *www.indiefilmhustle.com/podcasts*
BPS Podcast: *www.bulletproofscreenwriting.tv/podcasts*
Inside the Screenwriter's Mind: *www.screenwritersmind.com*
Filmtrepreneur Podcast: *www.filmtrepreneur.com/podcasts*
Filmmaking Motivation Podcast: *www.indiefilmhustle.com/fmpodcast*

IFH Podcast Network:

The IFH Podcast Network makes it easy for you to discover, connect, and engage with industry-leading filmmaking and screenwriting podcasts, all in one place. We curate the best podcasts that will help you on your filmmaking and screenwriting journey. You can listen to any of our shows on your favorite podcast platform. #IndieFilmUnite
www.ifhpodcastnetwork.com

Rise of the Filmtrepreneur

If you want to learn how to turn your filmmaking passion into a sustainable business my second book *Rise of the Filmtrepreneur: How to Turn Your Independent Film into a Profitable Business* will guide you on that path.

It's harder today than ever before for independent filmmakers to make money with their films. From predatory film distributors ripping them off to huckster film aggregators who prey upon them, the odds are stacked against the indie filmmaker.

The old distribution model for making money with indie film is broken and there needs to be a change. The future of independent filmmaking is the entrepreneurial filmmaker or the Filmtrepreneur®.

In *Rise of the Filmtrepreneur®* author and filmmaker Alex Ferrari breaks down how to actually make money with independent film projects and shows filmmakers how to turn their indie films into profitable businesses. This is not all theory, Alex uses multiple real-world case studies to illustrate each part of his method.

This book shows you the step by step way to turn your filmmaking passion into a profitable career. If you are making a feature film, series or any kind of video content, The Filmtrepreneur® Method will set you up for success. You can purchase the ebook, paperback or audiobook at *www.filmbizbook.com*

I hope to see you out in the world following your dream, the right way of course. And remember, stay away from gangsters who want to make feature films; there are easier ways to break into the film business, I'm just saying.

Special Thanks

My Wife: I would like to thank my wife, Maricruz Ferrari, who has been my partner throughout the ups and downs of chasing a filmmaking dream. I couldn't do it without her. I love you.

Connie H. Deutsch: The guidance, support, and love you have shown me throughout my life is something that will take multiple lifetimes to repay. Thank you.

Boris *(not his real name)*: My friend, without you hounding me for so many years this story wouldn't have been written. You were there for me in my darkest time, and I will never forget that. Thank you, and I owe you an espresso.

Frank *(not his real name)*: Your kindness to a young and scared film-maker helped me through this difficult time in my life. I will never forget you, my friend. Rest in peace.

Dan Cregan: Brother, you have been with me on this crazy ride for over a decade. You are a true friend. Thank you for always being there to lend a helping hand. BROKEN for life!

The Indie Film Hustle Tribe: Every day, you all give me the strength to keep doing the work I need to do. Thank you for all the support, and as always, keep that hustle going and keep that dream alive.

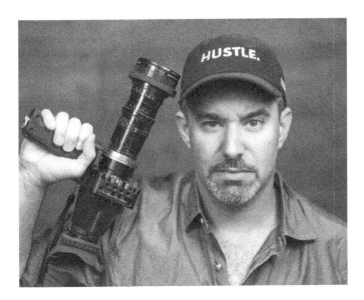

Alex Ferrari is an author, blogger, speaker, consultant, the host of the *Webby Award* Nominated and #1 filmmaking podcast on Apple Podcast *Indie Film Hustle Podcast*. He is an award-winning writer/director with 25 years of experience in the film industry. As a director, his films have screened in over 500 international film festivals. His latest feature film *On the Corner of Ego and Desire* World Premiered at the Raindance Film Festival in the UK.

Alex is also the founder of *IndieFilmHustle.com*, an industry-leading resource for filmmakers and screenwriters. He's also the host of the popular screenwriting based *Bulletproof Screenwriting Podcast*.

He recently launched *Filmtrepreneur.com*, a website/podcast/platform dedicated to showing filmmakers and creatives how to actually make money with their films. It's based on Alex's second book *Rise of the Filmtrepreneur: How to Turn Your Indie Film into a Moneymaking Business,* which rocketed to the top of the Amazon charts and became a #1 Best Seller within 10 hours of its release.

After launching Indie Film Hustle, Alex decided to create the world's first streaming service dedicated to filmmakers, screenwriters, content creators and artists called *Indie Film Hustle TV (IFHTV)*. He also launched the *IFH Academy*, a premiere online filmmaking and screenwriting education platform.

Alex currently lives in Los Angeles with his lovely family. He is a devoted practitioner of meditation and how it aids in the creative and business process. He also speaks regularly at screenwriting and film events, festivals and conventions.

Made in United States
North Haven, CT
21 September 2023